VINTAGE WEDDINGS

RESOURCE AND GUIDEBOOK

1910s-1950s

DANIELA TURUDICH

STREAMLINE PRESS

Published by
Streamline Press
1535 E. 3rd Street
Long Beach, California 90802
www.streamlinepress.com
customerservice@streamlinepress.com

First Edition
ISBN 1-930064-02-0

Other fine books from Streamline Press are available from your local bookstore or direct from publisher.

EVERY EFFORT HAS BEEN MADE to trace and acknowledge all copyright holders. Streamline Press and the author would like to apologize if any credit omissions have been inadvertently made. If brought to our attention, we will gladly make changes to any subsequent editions.

Illustrations on page: 45, © Victoria Fisk Couture

Distributed to the book trade by IPG, Chicago.

Printed by Transcontinental Printing, CANADA.

CONTENTS

INTRODUCTION

The word "vintage" literally means classic.

Having a vintage wedding means that the you'll get a classically stylish wedding with a little historical flare thrown in for good measure. You'll also get the satisfaction of knowing that your wedding will look and be different from all of the other weddings being planned this year.

This is not a wedding planner (although you will find a bridal checklist in the Odds and Ends chapter); rather it's a book on how to incorporate all the little things that will make a typical wedding into a classic vintage event. There's tons of information provided within these pages, but the book will primarily concentrate on the most important aspects that will turn a regular wedding into a *vintage* one.

We'll spend lots of time talking about wedding fashions from each decade along with the accessories worn. Much of the book will also concentrate on decorating ideas, flowers and color palettes. These aspects are very important if you're planning on creating a vintage atmosphere at your wedding or reception location. I've also included song lists from each era and tips on creating vintage invitations and thank you notes.

Whether you're planning a formal event or a casual affair, a vintage touch will add a little history and fun to the event. We thought it might be fun for those of you planning weddings to see how things were done during the first half of the Twentieth Century. At the same time, you'll get some practical ideas for invoking touches that will create a vintage atmosphere, regardless of time period.

We don't expect you to stick to what the book says word for word. We want you to be creative; take, leave, and modify the ideas presented within to suit your individual tastes and needs. All the ideas and suggestions given in this book …are just that. If you don't like a style – change it or modify it, if you don't like a recipe or menu – don't use it. And, if you want to mix and match periods – go for it, it's *your* wedding.

Daniela Turudich

GENERAL GUIDELINES

DRESS
What you wear plays an important part, whether you are planning a formal or informal wedding. A period atmosphere for your wedding isn't complete without the bride and groom in period or period-style attire. The outfits that you and the bridegroom wear will set the general tone of the wedding. You'll find four whole chapters on clothing and accessories.

Formal or informal attire is set by both personal preference and your choice of venue. Semiformal or informal attire looks best in garden settings, while formal dress is more appropriate in places of worship.

A NOTE ABOUT DRESS
Remember, these are just general guidelines. You should wear what makes you feel most comfortable.

WEDDING AND RECEPTION VENUES
The look and ambiance of your venue will greatly affect the overall look of your vintage wedding. Creating a vintage atmosphere is much easier when you have a historic or period venue. Otherwise, you'll have to make an extra effort to create the atmosphere needed for a vintage wedding. Decorating ideas and tips can be found in Chapter 5.

FLOWERS
Flowers play a large role in weddings. Period flower arrangements and bouquets will help create your vintage atmosphere. Popular flowers from each decade along with period bouquet ideas can be found in Chapter 3. Ideas for decorating using period flower arrangements can be found in Chapter 5.

COLOR SCHEME & DECORATIONS
Your color scheme and how you decorate will play a major role in creating a vintage look for your wedding. Wedding colors have changed significantly since the first half of the Twentieth Century, so color choice is very important. As far as how to decorate, ideas and tips on how to create a period look can also be found in Chapter 5.

TRANSPORTATION
Your choice of transportation for getting to and from the wedding, can also be used to create a vintage ambiance. Consider a vintage sedan or sports car for your bridal party. For the bride and groom, a vintage Rolls Royce or Bentley is the ultimate in elegance.

MUSIC
The type of music you play will be the single most determining factor in creating a vintage wedding. Music should be played from the decade you're trying to recreate. Music lists for each decade can also be found in Chapter 5.

CHAPTER 1
VINTAGE BRIDE

EARLY TWENTIETH CENTURY

1910s
pg 25

1920s
pg 31

1930s
pg 37

WEDDING FASHION TIMELINE

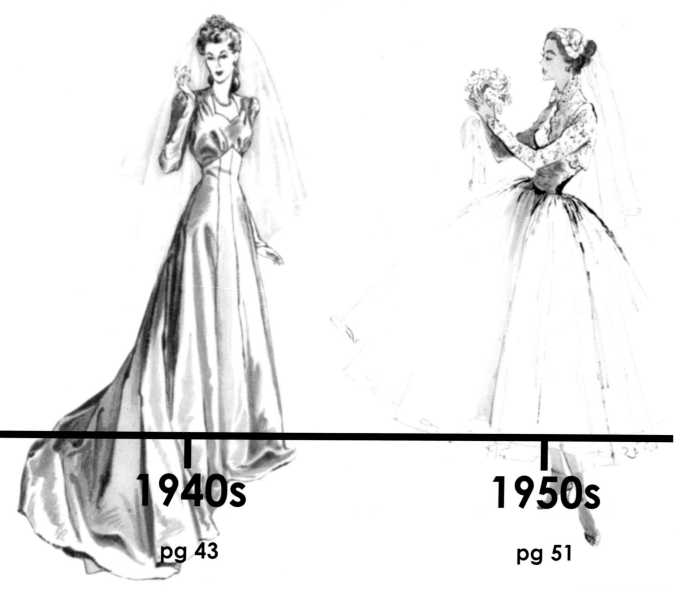

1940s

pg 43

1950s

pg 51

WHICH DRESS IS RIGHT FOR YOU?

Unless you're planning on wearing your grandmother's wedding gown, you'll have to search for the perfect vintage or vintage styled wedding dress. A vintage wedding is just not complete without the bride in a period or period style gown. It's quite all right if the period of the wedding dress doesn't match up with the period of the wedding, but a vintage dress that matches is preferable. No matter what era you'd like your wedding to be, you should try and find a dress that will flatter your good points and hide your imperfections.

Whether you want a vintage or new wedding gown, make sure to try on lots of different styles. Dresses that you would never imagine wearing have a funny way of looking great once they're tried on. It may also turn out that the 1940s wedding dress you've always pictured yourself in does nothing for your figure, while a 1950s dress may accentuate your every curve.

Antique stores, vintage clothing stores, and the web are all great resources for finding vintage dresses. For those of you who want a brand new dress, modern bridal salons are also a great resource. You'll be able to find brand new dresses that have been designed with a period look.

The goal is to find *the* wedding dress that will make you look and feel beautiful. You will know it when you find it. In the next few pages are some guidelines that will help you choose what type of dress will look best on you. It's important to remember that these are just guidelines and not hard and fast rules.

WEDDING GOWN SILHOUETTES

A-LINE/PRINCESS CUT

This silhouette is commonly found in wedding dresses of the **late 1930s** and throughout the **1940s**. This type of silhouette tends to look good on everyone. It's fitted in the bodice and then flares out at the waistline. It works great to camouflage hips, buttocks, and thighs. Needless to say, many women love this style.

EMPIRE

This silhouette was popular in the **1910s**. The empire silhouette has the waistline right under the breasts and flows down from there. This style works great to camouflage thick waists.

BALL GOWN/BELL SHAPE

This silhouette is typical of the **1950s**. The ball gown has a tight fitted bodice and a very full skirt. A petticoat is worn under the skirt to create a billowy bell shape. The pouffier the petticoat, the bigger the skirt. This type of silhouette is great for accentuating the bust and waist while drawing attention away from the hips and buttocks.

SHEATH

If the sheath goes straight up and down, like a chemise dress, then it is typical of the **1920s**. If the sheath is cut on the bias (makes the fabric stretchy and clingy) then it is typical of the **1930s**. The sheath silhouette tends to look best on petite women and or women with an hourglass figure.

NECKLINES

HIGH COLLAR

High collars are typical of both the early **1910s** wedding dresses and the fitted jackets worn over weddings gowns in the **1950s**. High collar necklines fit close to the neck and offers the bride tons of coverage and support.

HALTER

Halter necklines can be found in gowns from the **1930s** and the **1950s**. Halter necklines accentuate the bust line and work nicely for medium busted women.

SWEETHEART

Characteristic of **1940s** wedding gowns. The sweetheart neckline forms a heart shape at the bust line.

OFF THE SHOULDER

This neckline can be found in **1950s** wedding gown styles. Off the shoulder necklines looks like a strapless gown with sleeves attached at the shoulders. This is one way to have an open neckline without wearing a strapless dress.

V- NECK

This neckline can be found from the **1910s** through the **1950s**. The V neckline adds emphasis to the bust area.

ROUNDED

This neckline can be found from the **1910s** through the **1950s**. Rounded necklines can vary in depth but generally work well for most bust types.

STRAPLESS

Most typically found in **1950s** wedding gowns. Strapless gowns tend to impart the look of a corseted torso and add emphasis to the bust line.

WAISTLINES

BASQUE

This waistline is typically found in **1940s** wedding dresses. A basque waistline starts at the hips and creates a V-shape in the center. This style works to minimize the hips. If the V shape was pointing in an upward direction, it would then be typical of the **1930s.**

DROPPED

This waistline is typical of the **1920s.** Dropped waistlines elongate the waistline end at the hip. This waistline does not look good on full figured women.

NATURAL

This waistline is typical of **all decades except for the 1920s.** The natural waistline is the most popular waistline and works well for the average figure.

VINTAGE VERSUS NEW

Once you've decided on having a vintage wedding, the next question is always whether you should a wear a new or a vintage gown. Well, it's really up to the individual and what they feel comfortable in. Many people feel a little odd about wearing a dress that someone else has been married in, while others have no problem with it.

There are alternatives for women that do not want pre-owned gowns. As mentioned earlier, dresses with period lines can be found among contemporary designs. In some cases where a likeable period wedding gown cannot be found, there really is no choice but to purchase a new dress or have one made for you.

VINTAGE

Wearing a fifty or a hundred year old gown makes you feel like you've put on a little piece of history. That feeling is part of what makes wearing a vintage gown hugely popular. The feeling is especially wonderful if the gown was your grandmother's or has been passed down through your family.

The fabric, craftsmanship, style, and originality of a vintage wedding dress have made wearing a vintage gown a viable alternative to modern wedding dresses. They also tend to be less expensive than a brand new or custom made gown.

Finding the perfect gown will take some time, patience, and perseverance. **You'll have to know what you're looking for and act quickly when you find one that suits your taste.** Chances are if you see one you like, it's one of a kind and won't be there for long. Although you'll probably be anxious to take it home, make sure that you try on the gown before purchasing it. This is very important for any wedding dress, especially vintage. Vintage gowns are *used* and may have faults. Put it on and check it over *very carefully* before dishing out the money. This is not always possible to do if you're ordering from the Internet or a store across the country. In these instances, make sure that the store is willing to take returns if the dress does not fit or lacks the advertised quality.

Wedding dresses become more fragile as they get older. The older the dress is, the more restoration it may need. You should expect satin to yellow with age, lace and netting to rip, thread to weaken, and beads and crystals to fall off. Restorations will have to be done if you decide to wear the dress. Depending on the overall condition of the wedding gown, the reinforcement of weak stitches might be all that's need. Other restoration efforts might include the replacement of fallen or weakly held on crystals and beading, or the replacement of torn lace. Make sure to have an experienced seamstress or garment restorer do the restorations for you.

If your dream gown really is in a state of decay, restoring the wedding dress could cost you more than purchasing a new one or having it replicated. To have it replicated you need to find an *experienced* pattern maker to take apart the garment and create a pattern from scratch. The pattern can then be taken to an *experienced* costumer or seamstress to have them replicate the dress.

BRAND NEW

It's becoming easier and easier to find contemporary wedding dresses with a vintage flair. Many modern bridal gown designers are coming out with gowns that mirror period lines. This creates hundreds of more options for finding the perfect period or period style dress. Cinched waist ballerina gowns reminiscent of the 1950s are possible to find in modern bridal salons, as are 1940s princess styles. As of yet, you will not be able to find modern gowns based on Edwardian or 1920s designs. You'll have to find an original, have one made, or just wing it.

CUSTOM MADE

Custom made gowns are great for the bride that wants a specific, one-of-a-kind dress. Custom design will end up costing you about the same as purchasing a new dress off the rack. If you've decided to go this route, please make sure that you find an *experienced* costume designer to create your gown. Make sure that you find an *experienced* designer that knows the differences between decades of fashion. You may go into the consultation asking for a 1930s biased cut mermaid gown and walk away with a straight 1960-ish looking sheath.

Your first step in having a gown custom made is to figure out what kind of dress you want. The second step is to find a picture that's closest to your idea. Looking through old magazines will give you tons to choose from. Finding a vintage pattern, photograph, or illustration of a dress will not only clarify the type of dress you want, but will also give your costumer a visual to work off of. If you have not found any patterns or illustrations that you like, then at least try and draw out the "basic idea" of the type of dress you're looking for.

THE 1910s

The popularity of the "Gibson" girl was dying out. Women were beginning to think more of comfort, and fashion responded with lighter fabrics, brighter colors, and looser styles. Hemlines inched upwards and lipstick was beginning to be worn. Actresses showed their legs and Theda Bera made vamping popular for five long years. Vaudeville, ballroom dancing, and the Ouija board kept people entertained.

Floating hotels, like the Titanic and the Lusitania, sank. The Model T made motoring popular and Kodak produced a camera for the masses. Some people believed that these were the happiest years of the Twentieth Century, but then we entered WW I.

THE 1910s SILHOUETTE

At the beginning of the 1910s, the silhouette was long, thin and constricting. By the mid 1910s, silhouette hemlines inched upward and had a full skirt. Towards the end of the decade, fashion silhouettes were again long and straight, but not as constricting as earlier in the decade.

Opposite Page.
Wedding Gown, circa 1916
An illustration of a typical wedding dress from the middle of the decade. The hemline is a little above ankle length and the skirt is tiered and full. The dress has a slightly higher than natural waistline, and is tied with a sash. The dress is worn with an extremely long cap-style veil, secured at the ears with orange blossoms.

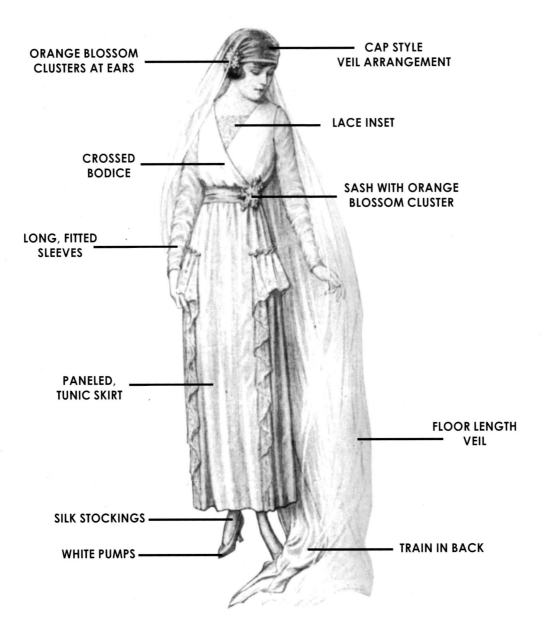

ORANGE BLOSSOM
CLUSTERS AT EARS

CAP STYLE
VEIL ARRANGEMENT

LACE INSET

CROSSED
BODICE

SASH WITH ORANGE
BLOSSOM CLUSTER

LONG, FITTED
SLEEVES

PANELED,
TUNIC SKIRT

FLOOR LENGTH
VEIL

SILK STOCKINGS

WHITE PUMPS

TRAIN IN BACK

THE 1910s WEDDING DRESS

Fashion and life style in the 1910s became much more relaxed than in previous decades. Waistlines were more natural and comfortable than the tightly corseted waists found earlier in the century.

Although women of the 1910s had given up the constricting Victorian corset, they adopted other confining fashions. Long narrow skirts, called hobble skirts (they restricted normal stride when worn), were at the height of fashion, early in the decade. Wedding dresses followed the hobble skirt trend during the early 1910s. The skirts were overlaid with material and then draped. This layering and draping of material created a "harem" skirt effect that was very popular. To see an illustration of this, flip to pages 28 and 29.

During the war years (1914-1918), hemlines inched upward and provided greater comfort. Wedding dresses became shorter and had full, tiered skirts. See illustration back on page 24.

After the war ended, fashions went back to long skirts with slender lines. Dresses during this time were made with flat, paneled tunic skirts, allowing for normal stride. See illustration to the left.

Opposite Page
Wedding Gown, circa 1918
The wedding gown is a common style from the latter part of the decade. The dress has a crossed bodice and a sash tied around the waist. The sash is fastened with an orange blossom cluster. The skirt is ankle length and has a train in back. The veil is worn cap-style and extends the length of the train.

Most wedding dresses were very elaborate throughout the decade. Dresses were white and draped or layered with gorgeous sheer and embroidered fabrics. Fabrics included satin, silk, chiffon, and velvet. Net fabric with embroidery or beading was also highly favored.

Trimmings for the wedding dress included a beautiful sash tied around the waistline. A cluster of orange blossoms would secure the sash in place. Also worn with the dress was a long flowing veil of net. The veil was most often worn cap-style and secured near the ears with clusters of orange blossoms. More information on veil styles and accessories can be found in Chapter 2.

Bridal Gown, circa 1913
The wedding dress consists of a hobble skirt with an overdress of embroidered material. The sleeves are long and fitted and the waist is tied with a sash. The sash is secured with a cluster of orange blossoms, which is typical of the era. The veil is long and worn cap-style with clusters of orange blossoms at the ears.

Waistlines throughout the decade were either Empire style or natural. Other common elements throughout the decade included long or slashed sleeves, watteu trains, and single or double crossed berthas.

Dresses constructed out of beaded georgette were popular for less formal weddings. For the informal war wedding, the bride often wore an afternoon dress of georgette, taffeta, or satin, and accessorized it with a dress hat.

Sample Bridal Gowns, circa 1913
Two gowns shown. **To the left:** *the dress has a natural waistline falling into a draped hobble skirt.* **To the right:** *the dress has an Empire waistline with a layered and draped skirt. Both women are wearing veils in cap-styles with a wreath of orange blossoms circling the head.*

THE 1920s

It was the time of Prohibition, bathtub gin, and the Charleston. The Jazz Age. Harlem had its renaissance and mobsters were powerful. Chaplin made us laugh, women swooned over Rudolph Valentino, and Clara Bow was the "it" girl. Hemlines rose again, women wore makeup, dressed like Parisian prostitutes ... and obtained the right to vote.

Art Deco was in style and everything was the cats pajamas – until the Depression hit in 1929.

THE 1920s SILHOUETTE

The silhouette was tube-like and loose. This was the decade of straight chemise dresses. Although the decade started out with some sort of waistline, it quickly disappeared by the mid 1920s.

Opposite Page.
Wedding Dress, circa 1928
This is an illustration of an ivory colored, satin wedding gown. The wedding gown has a fitted bodice, long pointed sleeves and a flowing skirt that lengthens gradually into a train. A tulle veil falls in folds from a bandeau worn low on the forehead.

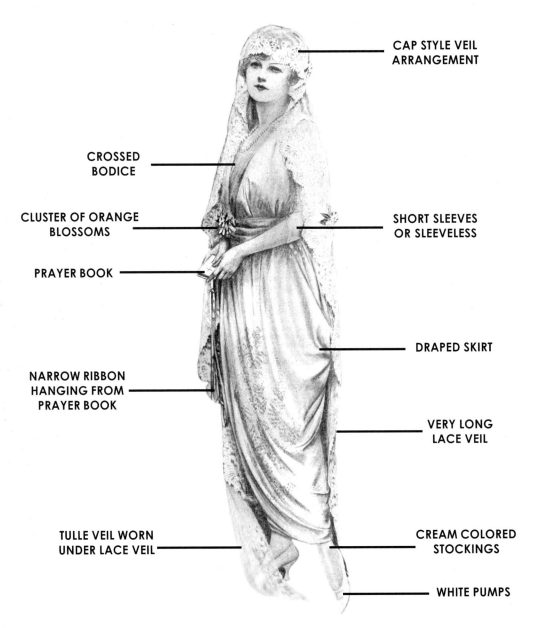

CAP STYLE VEIL
ARRANGEMENT

CROSSED
BODICE

CLUSTER OF ORANGE
BLOSSOMS

PRAYER BOOK

SHORT SLEEVES
OR SLEEVELESS

DRAPED SKIRT

NARROW RIBBON
HANGING FROM
PRAYER BOOK

VERY LONG
LACE VEIL

TULLE VEIL WORN
UNDER LACE VEIL

CREAM COLORED
STOCKINGS

WHITE PUMPS

THE 1920s WEDDING DRESS

During the beginning of the decade, wedding dresses were ankle length and had a waist at the natural waistline. Skirts were made slightly full. An example of this can be seen at the bottom right of this page. Some dresses even copied the draped "harem" skirts of the 1910s. This can be seen in the illustration on the opposite page at the left.

Fashion of the 1920s also adopted other elements from the 1910s. These included the extremely long veil worn, crossed bodice, and sashed waist.

In 1923 and 1924, waistlines dropped to the hips. By 1925 the waistline was completely discarded. During this time, hemlines inched upwards and dresses became the straight-hanging, short chemise that would characterize the era. Around 1928, waistlines started to reemerge and fashion began the trend towards the body-clinging styles that would characterize the 1930s.

Opposite Page.
Draped Wedding Dress, circa 1922
A nice example of a tunic dress made of satin that is hiked up onto one hip and secured with a bundle of fabric flowers. A veil of lace is draped over the head and worn cap-style.

This Page.
Informal Wedding Dress, circa 1920
An example of an early 1920s casual wedding dress. This is a short dress of white organdy with a rolling neckline. The skirt is full and layered. A white hat with lace trimmings is worn to accessorize.

Most wedding dresses throughout the decade were constructed as chemise dresses (a loose straight-hanging, one piece dress). A sheer overdress would then be worn over the chemise dress.

Chemise dresses were made of crepe, satin, chiffon, organdy, or silk. The sheer overdresses were made of net or chiffon and decorated with crystals, seeds, embroidery, or lace.

Tiered Wedding Dress, circa 1922
The illustration shows a tiered wedding dress made with a scalloped fichu collar. The fichu collar is secured in the front with a broach. The skirt mirrors the scallops at the neckline by having scalloped tiers of fabric down to the hemline. A long veil is worn with a bandeau of orange blossoms.

Neckline styles for the wedding dresses ranged from wide rolling berthas to lace trimmed fichus. Most dresses were sleeveless or had small puffed sleeves. Long fitted sleeves were reserved for more formal weddings.

The long cap-style veil was standard throughout the decade. The veil was usually attached to a bandeau worn low on the forehead, stopping right above the eyebrows. Further description on veil styles can be found in Chapter 2.

Wedding Dress, circa 1926
This is a great illustration showing the popular short skirt wedding dress of the mid 1920s. The veil is still worn very long and is secured with a low bandeau.

THE 1930s

The Depression. Millions of people were out of jobs and prohibition was repealed just in time. FDR's new deal brought some relief and Hollywood musicals brought hope. Streamlined designs made everything look modern and aerodynamic.

Everyone was scrimping and saving while Hollywood spent millions on movies. Fashion made women's clothing clinging and sensual. Jean Harlow wowed us with platinum blonde hair and kids were learning to Jitterbug and Lindy Hop. By the end of the decade things started to look up, and then the world entered a second war …

THE 1930s SILHOUETTE

The silhouette for most of the decade was long and thin with a fishtail-like train. Towards the end of the decade the silhouette changed to more of a princess line, but still emphasized the contours of the body.

Opposite Page.
Wedding Portrait, circa 1939
The bride in the photograph is wearing a headdress with a nice art deco design. She is also wearing a fitted satin jacket, buttoned down the front, over a satin evening dress.

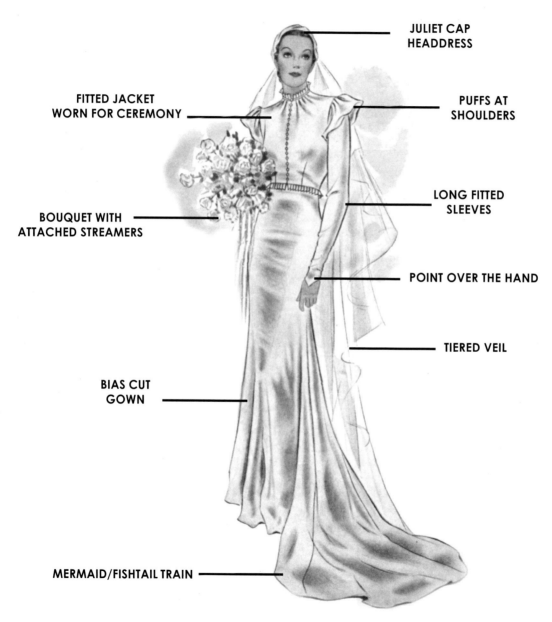

JULIET CAP
HEADDRESS

FITTED JACKET
WORN FOR CEREMONY

PUFFS AT
SHOULDERS

LONG FITTED
SLEEVES

BOUQUET WITH
ATTACHED STREAMERS

POINT OVER THE HAND

TIERED VEIL

BIAS CUT
GOWN

MERMAID/FISHTAIL TRAIN

THE 1930s WEDDING DRESS

The 1930s brought back the waistline and ushered in biased cut gowns. Women were ready for them after the boyish lines of the 1920s. Gowns cut on the bias of the fabric stretch nicely while accentuating every curve. The bias cut trend lasted the entire decade.

Wedding dresses also turned toward the bias cut, creating a slim and sensual line. Wedding dresses accentuated the body, flaring out at the hemline into a mermaid-like train. Bias cut wedding dresses were the standard, up until the late 1930s.

Opposite Page.
Wedding Gown, circa 1936
Gown is bias cut and is made of crisp, white silk taffeta. Over the gown is a short, fitted jacket of the same material. After the ceremony, the jacket is removed to show off the sleeveless evening gown underneath. The jacket buttons up in the front and has small puffs at the top of fitted sleeves.

The same gown may be modified for a less formal wedding by making it trainless and of white or pale pink organdy. Instead of the veil, an organdy hat would be worn.

This Page.
Informal Wedding Dress , circa 1930
The dress is made of chiffon in a soft rosy beige color. It is cut along flowing lines and has small puff sleeves ("decidedly 1930") made of matching lace. The skirt is tulip shaped. The dress is accessorized with a beige straw hat. Other accessories for this wedding dress would include beige suede gloves, beige kid leather shoes, a pearl buckle, and a pearl necklace.

Very late in the decade, wedding dress fashions made a move towards the princess/A-line silhouette that would characterize all wedding dresses of the 1940s. Also, for a short time in the late 1930s, wedding dresses had huge ruffled skirts. This was inspired by the release of the movie, *Gone With the Wind*.

At this time, peplums also made their debut. Like the A-line silhouette, peplums would come to characterize the 1940s wedding dress.

Most 1930s wedding gowns were made with lush fabrics to add richness to otherwise simple designs. Gowns would be made of silk, velvet, or satin and would often have interesting textures added with brocade or lace. But, simple gowns made of heavy satin were most popular and characterized the decade.

Wedding Dress, circa 1933
This gown is a beautiful example of a bias cut dress made with textured material of brocaded satin. The dress has slim, fitted sleeves and puffs at the shoulders. The dress is worn with a floor length veil that is attached to a slim head band.

Though they were simple, necklines were anything but boring. Necklines plunged into round or V-shaped fronts dipped dangerously low in the back. Cowl necklines were also very popular.

Dress hemlines grazed the ankle and stayed there until the end of the decade. Skirts were created to be slimming while flaring out into a mermaid's train at the hemline. To help emphasize slimness at the hips, skirts were constructed with V-shaped yokes extending from hip to hip.

Veils during the 1930s stayed long as in the 1910s and 1920s. The change came in how the veils were arranged. During the 1930s, veils were worn back and away from the face. They were attached to fitting head bands or Juliet caps. More information on veil styles can be found in Chapter 2.

Casual weddings during this time called for a slimming afternoon dress with a tulip shaped skirt. The dress would be accessorized with a hat.

Semiformal Wedding Dress, circa 1932
The gown shown is very appropriate for a semiformal garden wedding. The gown is made of net and chiffon. It has ruffles of net down the length of the skirt, but is still able to maintain the popular slim silhouette of the 1930s. The gown is sleeveless and is worn with opera-length gloves of net. A white net juliet cap is worn without a veil to promote the simplicity of the dress.

THE 1940s

We were in WW II. There were scrap drives, rationing of food supplies, and Victory gardens. Women were given blow torches and overalls. Kids were still dancing the Jitterbug. Women drew lines up the backs of their legs with eyeliner when stockings were rationed. Kilroy was here.

WW II ended and Christian Dior introduced the New Look. Commercial television became available to the public and then the Cold War began.

THE 1940s SILHOUETTE

The A-line/princess line was the standard silhouette for wedding dresses in the 1940s. The A-line silhouette lasted until Dior ushered in the "New Look" towards the end of the decade.

Opposite Page.
Bride and Flower Girl, circa 1943
Bride's dress is brocade and has the typical sweetheart neckline popular during the decade. Orange blossom clusters are still worn in the hair and the veil is draped over the head in a mantilla fashion. The flower girl wears a white dress with puffed sleeves.

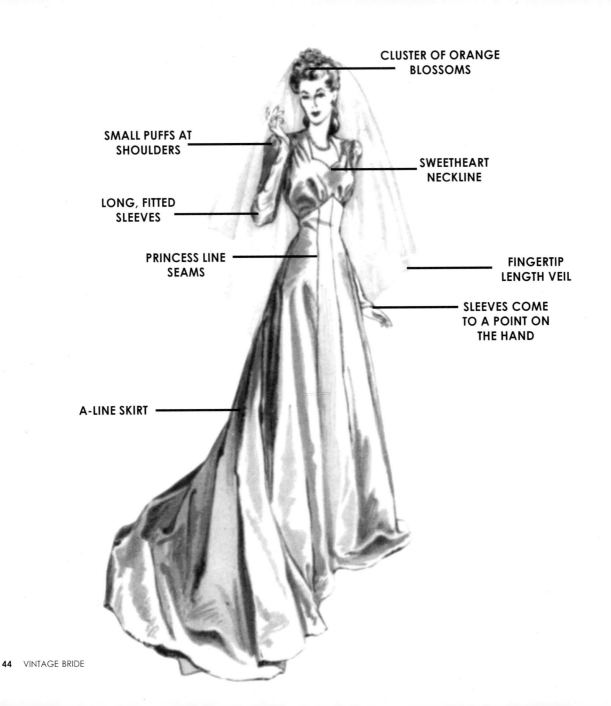

CLUSTER OF ORANGE
BLOSSOMS

SMALL PUFFS AT
SHOULDERS

SWEETHEART
NECKLINE

LONG, FITTED
SLEEVES

PRINCESS LINE
SEAMS

FINGERTIP
LENGTH VEIL

SLEEVES COME
TO A POINT ON
THE HAND

A-LINE SKIRT

THE 1940s WEDDING DRESS

The second world war consumed most of the 1940s. Men were being shipped off, while on the home front items were being rationed left and right. Weddings tended to be more casual and were usually planned in a hurry. In keeping with the spirit of the times, wedding dresses tended to be less formal than in previous decades. A nice afternoon dress worn with gloves and a hat was just fine for a rushed wedding.

The wartime trend did not prohibit long-length trains or veils, but these things were definitely not the norm, especially with the shortages and rationing. Wedding fashion guidelines advocated simplicity in line and trimming. The most popular gown tended to be of rayon-satin worn in an unadorned A-line style. Although simplicity was key, wedding dresses were anything but boring. Just look at the examples on the following pages.

Opposite Page.
Vintage Wedding Dress, circa 1943
This vintage wedding dress illustration shows the popular princess line silhouette and sweetheart neckline. The dress has long, fitted sleeves with small puffs at the shoulders. The veil is fingertip length and is adorned with orange blossoms.

This Page.
Wedding Suit, circa 1947
A suit, like the one shown, would be worn for an informal or rushed wedding. Gloves and a small hat would have been worn as accessories.
Designed by Victoria Fisk Couture.

The A-line dress, also called the princess line, had a fitted bodice, and an A-line skirt. Peplums at the waist were also very popular.

Wedding dresses were usually constructed out of rayon-satin. For those brides who wanted a little something different, over-skirts of sheer netting and fabric would create a soft billowy effect. Also popular were skirts made of net with satin flower appliques and skirts with ruffles.

Moderate length veils were worn with decorative headdresses. More information on veil styles can be found in Chapter 2.

Wedding Gown, circa 1943
The dress pictures is made of exquisite satin and has lace appliques at the neckline. This is great example of an A-line dress worn with a fingertip length veil.

A-line dresses with sweetheart necklines lasted until 1947, when the "New Look" emerged. Following the new fashion trend, wedding dresses took on a bell shape that would characterize 1950s wedding gowns. Please refer to the 1950s wedding dress section for bell shaped styles.

Wedding Gown, circa 1943
This gown is made of white rayon satin, delicately yoked in net with appliqued lace scoring at the neckline. The dress also has a wonderful peplum and long fitted sleeves.
Designed by Holmes.

WW II WEDDINGS

Where can we have a small reception at the army camp?

If your fiancé is an officer, the reception can take place at the officers' club or at a local hotel or country club. If he is a noncommissioned officer or private, it can take place at the N.C.O.'s club or at a service club.

My fiancé is a private, his best friend has a commission. Can the officer be in the wedding party?

For the private or non-com, no. For a commissioned officer, yes.

Who walks under the arch of swords?

Only the bride and groom may pass under the traditional arch of swords.

What about dress?

Full dress uniforms for the army and navy are in moth balls for the duration. Therefore the army groom wears the olive drab field service uniform and the navy man wears his service uniform. A service bride married from home has a choice of elaborate or simple dress but for a camp or navy station wedding, a daytime dress or suit is favored.

An excerpt from "What's What for Military Weddings," By Nancy Shea.

Woman's Home Companion, 1942

Opposite Page.
Military Wedding Photograph, circa 1942
The bride and groom cut the cake, as a guest toasts the newlyweds.

THE 1950s

The economy was good. People were buying new houses, new appliances, and beautiful new gas-guzzling cars. Some women worked, but most stayed home. Women threw Tupperware parties and made Hawaiian punch. Plastic was the "wonder material." Bobby soxers abounded, Bill Haley and the Comets kept us rocking, and Elvis was king. Fashion saw the tight sweater look (inspired by Marylin), poodle skirts, pencil skirts, crinoline, Lucite heels, and saddle shoes.

People were scared of the Atomic bomb, built bomb shelters, and watched out for Communists…but overall the decade had a sweet sense of innocence.

THE 1950s SILHOUETTE

The bell-shape was the silhouette of the 1950s wedding gown. It combined a tight tiny torso with a full skirt that ballooned out at the waistline. Everything from the bodice to the accessories was tiny and fitted, except for the large, billowy skirt. The innocent ballerina-princess silhouette was the look of the decade.

Opposite Page
Wedding Dress, circa 1952
The photograph illustrates a great example of a bell shaped gown. A strapless satin gown is worn under an overdress of lace and netting. The peter pan collar of the overdress is very typical of the era.

LACE HALF-CAP

SMALL NOSEGAY BOUQUET WITH HANGING BOW

FITTED JACKET WITH PETER PAN COLLAR OVER A STRAPLESS DRESS

TIGHT, FITTED JACKET SLEEVES

SMALL, CINCHED WAIST

FINGERTIP LENGTH VEIL

FULL, BELL SHAPED SKIRT MADE WITH LAYERS OF TULLE. SKIRT SHOWN IS BALLERINA LENGTH. FLOOR LENGTH WAS ALSO COMMON.

FULL PETTICOATS WORN UNDERNEATH SKIRT

SANDAL-FOOT SILK STOCKINGS

WHITE, STRAPPY SANDALS

THE 1950s WEDDING DRESS

Fit was everything in 1950s wedding dresses. Bodices were tucked and fitted. Waists were cinched into waif-like thinness with huge skirts ballooning out from under them. This combination made the bride seem as if she weighed nothing and could be blown away by a sudden gust of wind.

The ballerina-princess shaped silhouette usually came in two popular dress lengths. The first was a classic and traditional floor length bell shaped gown, with or without a train. See an illustration of this back on page 50. The second was a sweet and charming ballerina length gown that stopped at the lower calf and looked like a long tutu. Illustrations of the ballerina length gown are shown on these two pages.

Opposite Page.
Ballerina Length Wedding Gown, circa 1952
The wedding gown.combines nylon tulle with imported Chantilly lace, etched with sequins and simulated pearls. It has a high-standing petal collar, sweeping skirt, and full train. It came in white, ivory, blush pink, or ice blue. The dress is accessorized with a shell cap of pleated netting (with lace appliques) and a fingertip length veil.
Dress designed by Maria of Pandora for Gimbels, New York.

This Page.
Informal Wedding Dress, circa 1953
Shown is an example of a shorter, ballerina length gown with tightly fitted bodice and short sleeves. The dress is worn with a short fitted jacket

An undergarment called a corselet was used to create the cinched waist. A corselet was a small corset that wrapped just around the waist area.

In order to achieve the bell shaped skirt, women had to invest in various undergarments. One such undergarment was called the bombast. The bombast was a very short taffeta petticoat that encircled the hips with small hoops. It was considered more efficient and graceful than wearing an A-line petticoat with a hoop at the hem. Over the bombast, women would wear one or two full petticoats gathered into a flat waistband. Over the petticoats would be added yet another petticoat. The last petticoat was supposed to be more glamorous and was often pastel colored. A woman could very reasonably end up having as many as four full layers of petticoats under one dress.

Top.
Bra-s'lette, circa 1955
Shown is a period strapless bra that cinches the waist as it lifts the breasts. Also shown is a short petticoat meant to give fullness at the hips. Fullness at the hips helped the skirt achieve a bell shape.

Bottom.
Hoop Skirt, circa 1955
A six-tiered hoop skirt such as this would have provided extra fullness underneath the bridal gown.

Wedding dress fabrics ranged from the more formal bridal satins to light tulles or organdies. Chantilly lace was also very fashionable. If the bride wasn't wearing it, the mother of the bride most certainly was.

During the decade, it was common for the wedding dress skirts to be made of layers of tulle. This imparted the "light as air" effect so popular during the decade.

Informal Ballerina Length Gown, circa 1951
The gown was made of nylon tulle and imported Chantilly lace. It came in the following colors: ice-blue, blush-pink, champagne, and white.
Made by Emily Fifth Avenue for The Career Girls Store.

Towards the middle of the decade, fashion saw the emergence of the dual-purpose wedding gown. Very often a wedding dress or bridesmaid's gown would consist of two different dresses or a dress and a fitted jacket. The overdress or jacket would be worn on top of a strapless dress for the ceremony and then removed for the reception. Normally, the fitted jacket would be sheer with a peter-pan collar and covered buttons up the front.

Wedding dresses of the decade had either really long fitted sleeves, short cap sleeves, or were completely strapless. Bridal headdresses included mantilla veils, crowns, or close-fitting caps with veils attached to the back. Bouquets tended to be somewhat small and were looked at as accessories rather than focal points.

Convertible Gown, circa 1951
The dress is ballerina length and made of nylon tulle and imported lace. The fitted jacket can be removed to reveal a strapless formal.
Made by Dey Bros. of Syracuse, New York.

...but I'll always love John Wanamaker!

John Wanamaker

PHILADELPHIA
WILMINGTON

*Wedding Gown, circa 1954
The wedding gown pictured,
shows just how tiny women's
waists were. The long fitted
bodice helps accentuate the
tiny waist. The waist is further
accentuated by having the
skirt start at the hip line. The
neckline is open and wide
with long fitted sleeves.
Gown designed by Gaston
Mallet of Murray Hamburger
exclusively for
John Wanamaker Bridal
Bureau.*

CHAPTER 2
BRIDAL ACCESSORIES

BRIDAL VEILS

Veiling is what makes a bride look like a bride. It is what makes people across the room see you, and know that you are the reason for them being there. Without it, you would just look like a pretty girl in a fancy dress.

It's important to note here that in order to create an authentic, vintage wedding ensemble, your veil arrangement should match your dress style. One simple rule to remember when thinking about veiling is: **The slimmer your dress – the longer and slimmer your veil should be. The pouffier your dress – the pouffier and shorter your veil should be.** Again, these are general guidelines, not hard and fast rules.

Veils were typically made of tulle or lace. Below are some simple veil length guidelines that were standard for each decade:

1910s – Veil was floor length or longer.

1920s – Veil was floor length or longer.

1930s – Veil was tiered, slimming, and extended the length of the gown.

1940s – Veil was fingertip or elbow length. These are still the most popular veil lengths.

1950s – Veil was elbow or flyaway length and very fluffy. The fluffiness of the veil matched the fullness of the dress.

Opposite Page.
Veil and Headdress, circa 1927
An example of a 1920s veil worn low on the forehead and secured with an embroidered bandeau.

1910s BRIDAL VEIL

Most brides wore bridal tulle, which came by the yard, three yards wide. The edges were either left raw or else finished with narrow lace or satin ribbon. The veil extended to the floor. If a train was worn, then it extended to the bottom of the train.

Most veils were arranged cap-style and secured with half-circle clusters of orange blossoms at the ears.

Above Right.
Bridal Veil, circa 1916
Tulle is arranged in cap style across the forehead and then gathered at the sides with orange blossoms.

Above Left.
Bridal Veil, circa 1915
Tulle is gathered and shirred into rows, creating a modified cap. Orange blossom clusters are attached at the sides.

Above Middle.
Bridal Veil, circa 1915
Tulle is gathered at the back of the head and fanned upward, leaving the rest to fall down the back. A bandeau of wax orange blossoms encircles the head.

1920s BRIDAL VEIL

Veils in the 1920s were made of tulle or lace and were worn over the head in cap-style. They were secured with bandeaus that were worn low on the forehead, ending just above the eyebrows. Bandeaus were decorated with wax orange blossoms or embroidered material. Veils extended to the floor or if a train was worn, to the end of the train.

Bridal Veils, circa 1922
From left to right: Lace is worn in a cap effect and gathered at the sides; lace is worn low on the forehead and draped over a high comb in the back; a coronet is worn low on the forehead securing the tulle veil in a cap effect.

1930s BRIDAL VEIL

During the 1930s, the length of the veil shortened and more attention was paid to the headdress. The veil and headdress were worn back and away from the face.

Headdresses consisted either of slim head bands or juliet caps. Both were simple designs that fit close to the head. Close fitting headdresses helped to emphasize the slim, elongated lines of 1930s fashion. During the late 1930s, mantilla veils (shown below) started to become popular.

Left.
Mantilla Veil, circa 1938
Lace draped over the head in mantilla fashion.

Above.
Headdress and Veiling, circa 1936
This is a nice example of a simple braided head band worn far off the face. The veiling is attached to the back of the band allowing for the fabric to fall away from the face.

1940s BRIDAL VEIL

Veils attached to decorative headdresses were standard for weddings. The veil was either fingertip or else elbow length. Decorative headdresses included tiaras and head bands. Many women also donned clusters of flowers as headdresses. Refer to page 73 for common vintage flowers.

If a headdress was not worn, tulle veiling could be arranged into a modified headdress. See examples on the following page.

Upper Left.
Tiara with Veiling, circa 1944
A tiara headdress of beads and pearls is worn high on the head. Veiling is attached to the back.

Bottom Near Right.
Tulle Headdress, circa 1940
A very cute look is made by gathering one end of the tulle into bunches creating a headdress and letting the rest of the tulle fall into a veil.

Bottom Far Right.
Headdress, circa 1941
Matching a heart-shaped headdress with the sweetheart neckline was also very popular in the 1940s.

INSTEAD OF A VEIL...
CIRCA 1944

A hurry-up wedding may change your plans for a long drifting veil and a satin gown. But you needn't give up the misty bridal look that a veil imparts. Here are five headdresses, especially designed to go with a short wedding dress and to make you a memory-book bride.

Upper Left. Attach streamers of tulle to a flower calot, tie a butterfly bow under your chin.

Upper Right. Sprinkle a white tulle band with crystal stars, finish with a huge bow and long floating streamers.

Bottom Left. Double a length of tulle and gather the folded end so it will stand up like a halo. Draw tulle around over the ears, knot it in back to form a turban. Trim with roses.

Bottom Middle. Drape soft lace to make a hood and shoulder cape. Fasten at the front with a handsome pin.

Bottom Right. Gather tulle to make a quaint hooded cap, drape end across the front and fasten with white violets.

1950s BRIDAL VEIL

Veils in the 1950s were short and billowy. Most were kept between elbow and flyaway length. Veils were attached to small, fitted headdresses. Popular headdresses of the era included coronets (crowns), juliet caps, and half-caps. Headdresses were worn farther back on the head, away from the face.

Below.
Bridal Caps, circa 1952
The woman in the foreground is wearing a half cap with attached veiling. The woman in the background is wearing a juliet cap with attached veiling.

Composite at Right.
Bridal Headdresses, circa 1955
Clockwise starting from upper right:
Close fitting head band; rhinestone coronet worn on top of the head; half-cap worn far back on the head; standing head band.

Your Dream — Your Veil

Juliet
BRIDAL
VEILS

UNDERGARMENTS

The look of your wedding dress will depend heavily on what you wear underneath it. Period gowns were always worn with some sort of "tight and tuck" device, and if you want to get the same look and line, you'll have to do the same. All period dresses were made to suit a particular figure line that changed from decade to decade. Below is a breakdown of decades and what body lines were popular.

1910s - Corseted waist and hips.

1920s - Flattened curves imparting a boyish figure. Busts, hips, and buttocks were all flattened.

1930s - Flattened tummy and hips; uplifted breasts. This imparted a slim and elongated look.

1940s - Curves were under control. Nothing was flattened. Rather, curves were smoothed and contoured.

1950s - Hourglass figure. Uplifted breasts, full hips, and a small cinched waist.

PRODUCTS USED FOR FLATTENING, LIFTING, AND CINCHING

CORSET – Used to cinch the waist and lift the breasts.

GIRDLE – Used to flatten the tummy and the hips.

BRAZIER – Used to flatten, uplift, or enhance the breasts. Strapless braziers may have built in girdles to lift while flattening the stomach.

PRODUCTS USED FOR ADDING VOLUME

BRAZIER – Padded braziers can be worn to add and enhance cleavage.

PETTICOATS – Petticoats are worn under skirts to add volume. A-line petticoats create an A-line shape, while petticoats full at the hips helps create a bell shape.

OTHER BRIDAL ACCESSORIES

Accessories are the little extras that makeup the overall look of the costume. The choice of accessories is important. In keeping with period tradition, your choice of accessories should be minimal and simple.

"Wear a gown that is sugared but not a confectioner's dream. Let simplicity be the keynote."
(Bride's Magazine Summer, 1943)

Just because you like the idea of having a certain accessory doesn't mean that your gown needs it. You only want to add accessories that are necessary to the overall look of your costume. On the following pages are listed some common accessories and explanations of when and when not to use them.

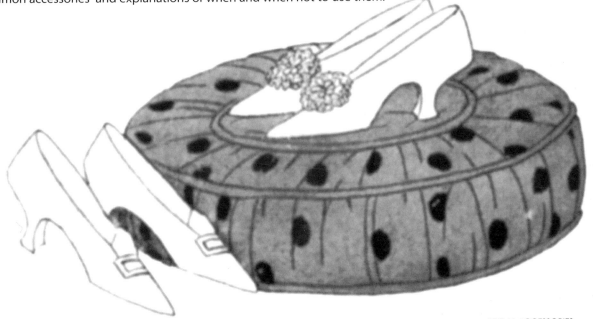

GARTER - *ALWAYS WORN*

The lucky blue garter was always lace frilled and could be ornamented with rosebuds or orange blossoms and tied with narrow ribbons.

GLOVES - *SOMETIMES WITH SHORT SLEEVES OR SLEEVELESS DRESSES*

Gloves are generally reserved for formal gowns that are sleeveless or have short sleeves. Period gloves were made of white kid leather or satin. Gloves are typically not worn for a garden wedding. If you really want to wear them for a garden wedding, make sure they're short and of lace or net. If you're wearing gloves that are elbow length or longer, they should be slightly crushed at the elbow joint to allow for movement.

HOSIERY - *ALWAYS WORN*

Stockings in the 1910s and 1920s were of white or cream colored silk. Starting with the 1930s and up through the 1950s, flesh or cream-colored stocking were popular. Stockings with a "sandal foot" are worn with wedding sandals.

JACKET - *SOMETIMES WITH SHORT SLEEVES OR SLEEVELESS GOWN*

Jackets should be small and fitted and worn over gowns with short sleeves or of a sleeveless variety. Bolero jackets were popular in the 1930s and 1950s. Sheer fitted jackets of net with buttons up the front were also popular during the 1950s.

JEWELRY - *ALWAYS WORN*

A single strand of pearls worn with the wedding gown is classically elegant. Pearl earrings to match would be fine also. Anything more should be carefully considered as it might be too much. Oh, and of course your wedding band.

SHOES - *ALWAYS WORN*

White pumps or sandals are standard. During the 1910s-1930s, shoes were trimmed with decorative accents such as white lace rosettes, orange blossoms clusters, buckles, and bows.

STOLES - *SOMETIMES WITH STRAPLESS GOWNS*

Tulle stoles are classically vintage and are worn with strapless gowns. These were very popular during the 1950s.

"RULE OF 14"

HOW TO KNOW WHEN YOU ARE SMARTLY DRESSED, CIRCA 1948

Everything you wear that's visible to others should add up to a total of not more than 14 pts. Count up the points below and compare it to the point chart. If you are wearing more than one of the same item, count it twice.

DRESS	1		BUCKLES	1
HAT	1		BOW	1
VEIL	1		EARRINGS	1
CLIP	1		BRACELET	1
FLOWER	1		RING	1
HOSE	1		HANDKERCHIEF	1
DARK HEELS	1		GLOVES	1
SANDALS	1		PURSE	1
PUMPS	1		WRAP OR JACKET	1

POINT TOTALS:

OVER DRESSED = Over **14** pts

SMARTLY DRESSED = **12** to **14** pts

UNDER DRESSED = **8** to **12** pts

VINTAGE WEDDING FLOWERS AND FOLIAGE

Here is a short list of the most popular flowers used in period weddings for both bouquets and decorations. Stars have been placed next to flowers and plants that were MOST popular for bouquets from the 1910s through the 1950s. If you can't decide, you'll never go wrong with using orange blossoms or lilies of the valley. Either choice is classically vintage.

Asparagus Fern

Buttercup

Calla Lily

*Carnation

Chrysanthemum

Daffodil

Daisy

Delphinium

Dogwood or cherry blossoms for decoration

Forget-Me-Not

Garden Flowers

Geranium

Heather

Iris

*Ivy

Lavender

Lily

*Lily of the Valley

Maiden Hair Fern

*Orange Blossom

*Orchid

Pansy

Petunia

Pink and White

Queen Anne's Lace

*Rose

Sweet Pea

Tulip

Violet

VINTAGE BOUQUET STYLES

ARM BOUQUET: A medium sized bouquet without streamers. Most popular in the **1930s** and **1940s**.

NOSEGAY BOUQUET: Small and round in shape. Popular in the **1930s** and the **1950s**.

PRAYER BOOK: A prayer book ornamented with streamers of ribbon with attached flowers. Popular throughout **all decades**.

SHOWER BOUQUET: A large or medium sized bouquet with streamers of ribbon with attached flowers falling from the bouquet. Most popular in the **1910s** and **1920s**.

SPRAY BOUQUET: A simple cluster of flowers, tied with a ribbon. Most popular in the **1930s**.

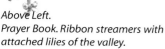

Above Left.
Prayer Book. Ribbon streamers with attached lilies of the valley.

Bottom Left. Nosegay Bouquet. Tiny roses, forget-me-nots and one deep pink rose make a quaint nosegay, charmingly set off with a frill of silver paper and a silver ribbon tied in a bow.

Above Right.
Nosegay Bouquet. Streamers with attached lilies of the valley.

Bottom Right. Spray Bouquet. Roses, delphinium, and stock tied together with colored gauze ribbon that matches the bridesmaid's dresses.

BOUQUET IDEAS BY PERIOD

The one basic rule that you should remember regarding bouquets: **The bigger the bouquet, the lighter the flower colors should be. The smaller the bouquet, the brighter or darker the flower colors can be.**

If you're planning on having a huge shower bouquet in the 1920s style, light or pastel colored flowers will help the bouquet accessorize with your dress. If you choose bright or dark colored flowers to be used in a large bouquet, all the attention will be drawn away from the dress and directly to your flowers. A big faux pas! Bouquets should never overpower your dress.

1910s & 1920s

The 1910s and 1920s used the same bridal bouquet arrangement. Bridal bouquets tended to be somewhat of a focal point and were very elaborate. Flowers were arranged in shower bouquets without much green filler. **Orange blossoms** or **lilies of the valley** were attached to ribbon streamers that hung from the bouquet. Attendants carried loose arm bouquet tied with a drooping bow.

FLOWERS FOR THE BRIDE'S BOUQUET

- White **orchids** or **roses** combined with **lilies of the valley**.
- **Lilies of the valley** and white **orchids**, with not too much green.
- A big loose bouquet of white **lilacs** or white **Easter lilies** tied with satin ribbon.
- Prayer book tied with white satin ribbon and hanging ribbon streamers.
- **Lilies of the valley** and **maidenhair fern** tied with white gauze ribbon.
- A cluster of white **freesias** and dark green leaves.
- A cluster of white **Easter Lilies**.
- White **sweet peas** and **gardenias**, with a drooping bow of white and silver ribbon.
- WW I military bouquet includes red **roses**, **lilies of the valley**, and **cornflowers**.

FLOWERS FOR AN ATTENDANT'S BOUQUET

- **Roses** and **sweet peas**.

- **Lilacs** combined with blue and yellow **pansies**.

- Nosegays of **mignonette** combined with **wild roses** or spicy old fashioned **pink and white pinks** from home.

1930s

During the 1930s we see a move away from the huge opulent bouquets of the 1920s. Flowers were arranged in spray bouquets or nosegays without much, if any green.

FLOWERS FOR THE BRIDE'S BOUQUET

- Long or short stemmed cluster of **calla lilies** tied with a satin bow.

- Long stemmed white **roses** tied with a satin bow.

- **Orange blossoms** and **lilies**.

- A cluster of **lilies of the valley** tied with a velvet or silk ribbon.

- Nosegay of small white **rosebuds**.

- Nosegay of **tiny roses** and **forget-me-nots**.

- Garland of white **roses** and **freesia** looped gracefully around the arm.

- Spray of **garden flowers**.

- **White stock** (any white flower) bouquet with unconventional sprays of pink and blue **delphinium**.

FLOWERS FOR AN ATTENDANT'S BOUQUET

- Yellow **snapdragons**, pale blue **delphinium**, and a few pink **African daisies**.

- **Roses** and **delphinium** tied with gauze ribbon.

- Cluster of **lilacs**.

1940s

The decades of large opulent bouquets ended with the start of WW II. The 1940s bride was anything but extravagant. Bouquets were kept small to medium in size. For the informal service wedding, a corsage of orchids was worn.

FLOWERS FOR THE BRIDE'S BOUQUET

- White **orchids** with **fern**.
- **Roses**.
- **Madonna lilies**.

FLOWERS FOR AN ATTENDANT'S BOUQUET

- **Delphinium**.
- Armfuls of **tiger lilies**.
- A cluster of **garden flowers**.

1950s

The 1950s wedding bouquet was the decidedly small nosegay, which acted only as an accessory to the beautiful bell-shaped gowns of the decade.

FLOWERS FOR THE BRIDE'S BOUQUET

- **Roses**.
- **Tulips** with the petals turned back.
- **Hyacinths** in stiff spiky nosegays.

FLOWERS FOR AN ATTENDANT'S BOUQUET

- Complimentary nosegays to the bride's bouquet.

CHAPTER 3
VINTAGE BRIDESMAIDS

BRIDESMAIDS

The most popular trend throughout the early Twentieth Century was to have all the bridesmaids wear a dress of the same color or shades of the same color. If there was a maid of honor, she was made to stand out from the rest of the bridesmaids. This would be done by making the maid of honor's dress a different color; it could be either a darker version of the bridesmaids' dresses, or of a contrasting color.

During the war years of the 1940s, the trend for variety of dress styles and colors continued as bridesmaids made do with nicer afternoon dresses worn for the informal war wedding. Beginning postwar and lasting into the 1950s, reasonably priced mass produced dresses allowed for bridesmaids to start dressing uniformly. The modern day notion that all of the attendants should wear the same *exact* dress came about during this time period.

Opposite Page.
Bridesmaids, circa 1925
This is a great illustration showing the typical straight chemise dresses of the era. These dresses are loosely tied about the hips with a sash and have ruffled layers toward the bottom. The dresses are worn with cloche hats trimmed with flowers.

This Page.
Best & Co. Advertisement, circa 1943
This is an illustration for a bridesmaid's two-piece dress from the 1940s. The top is belted and has peplums draped over an A-line skirt. A snood is worn in the hair as an accessory.

A QUICK GUIDE TO BRIDESMAID'S ACCESSORIES

HAIR ACCESSORIES

1910s – Large picture hats trimmed with flowers, ribbons, and plumes.

1920s – Cloche, fitted cap, or poke bonnet.

1930s – Turbans or wide-brimmed hats.

1940s – Hats, flowers, or snoods.

1950s – Flowers or small, fitted hats.

GLOVES

Gloves should be worn with short sleeved or sleeveless dresses only. Other than that, it's up to personal preference. However, if one bridesmaid is wearing them, all of them should.

SHOES

Sandals or pumps are dyed to match the color of the dress.

STOCKINGS

Flesh colored stockings are worn.

STOLE

Wraps or stoles are worn with sleeveless or strapless dresses only.

Bridesmaid, circa 1930
The bridesmaid's dress is printed chiffon and has a tulip shaped skirt. The dress is accessorized with a turban and shoes to match.

1910s BRIDESMAIDS

Bridesmaid's gowns usually mirrored both the current fashion trends and the bride's gown. The gowns were usually made of georgette, printed chiffon, crepe, taffeta, satin, net, organdy, or cotton voile. Large picture hats made of georgette, tulle, straw, or chiffon were worn as an accessory to the dress. Hats were trimmed with flowers, ribbon, and ostrich plumes.

Bridesmaids carried loose arm bouquets tied with a drooping bow. Flower choices for the bridesmaids bouquets were chosen to match the color scheme of the wedding. See page 75 for bouquet ideas.

If the wedding was informal, the bride would have only one attendant.

Bridesmaids Gown, circa 1910
The bridesmaids gown shown is of a hobble skirt variety with a band encircling the knees for restricted movement. The dress has a square neckline and is tied with a sash at the waist. The dress is paired with a large picture hat trimmed with roses and plumes.

1920s BRIDESMAIDS

Bridesmaid's gowns of the 1920s followed hemline trends throughout the decade. Early in the 1920s, when there was still a waistline present, bridesmaids wore dresses made of organdy or dotted Swiss. These dresses had quaint wide skirts, puff sleeves, and round necklines. The dresses were accessorized with wide brimmed bonnets. An illustration of an early 1910s dress can be seen below left.

During the mid 1920s, bridesmaids wore fashionable straight chemise dresses with cloche hats. A nice illustration of this can be found back on page 80.

In the late 1920s bridesmaid's dresses became longer and more full. An example of this can be seen at the right.

Left.
Bridesmaid's Dress, circa 1921
This bridesmaid's frock has a skirt ruffled from hem to belt. It has a small bodice with a demure fichu. Short-ruffled sleeves complete the effect. It is accessorized with a flower-trimmed poke bonnet.

Right.
Bridesmaid's Dress, circa 1928
This dress has a slight waistline, and a long full skirt. A skirt of netting is worn over a shorter, lace trimmed dress. The dress is sleeveless and is accessorized with a wide brimmed, droopy hat.

1930s BRIDESMAIDS

The princess silhouette with a tulip shaped skirt typifies bridesmaid's gowns from this era. Tulip shaped skirts created fullness at the hemline without adding extra width to the skirt.

During the 1930s, the trend for the dual-purpose bridesmaid's dress came into being. This was most likely in direct response to the hardships of the Depression.

Most bridesmaid's dresses were made either sleeveless or with short sleeves. Over the dress would be worn either a small cape or bolero jacket. Once the ceremony was over, capes and jackets were removed to reveal hidden evening gowns underneath.

For a brief time during the late 1930s (right after *Gone With the Wind* was released) bridesmaids wore huge pouffy skirts with petticoats underneath.

Bridesmaid's Dresses, circa 1936
The dresses have a pale blue net over blue taffeta. Under the cape is a low-necked evening dress. The dresses are accessorized with straw hats.

An illustration of an earlier 1930's bridesmaid's dress can be found back on page 82.

1940s BRIDESMAIDS

During the war years and times of strict rationing, bridesmaid's dresses would often consist of nice A-line afternoon frock. An afternoon frock could be dressed up with gloves, flowers and jewelry to make it more appropriate for the informal war wedding.

For more formal weddings, bridesmaids wore A-line blouse and skirt sets. Blouses were either belted with peplums or tucked into tiny waisted dirndl skirts (a full skirt with a tight waistband).

At the end of the decade, bridesmaid's dress started to take on an hourglass shape (full, A-line dresses with tiny cinched waists). The hourglass shaped silhouette would come to characterize 1950's fashion.

Right.
Informal Bridesmaid, circa 1944
A young bridesmaid, probably the only attendant, wears a nice afternoon dress. The dress is accessorized with darker elbow length gloves and matching shoes. Her hair is adorned with flowers that match her bouquet. An illustration of a more formal 1940's bridesmaid's dress can be found back on page 81.

1950s BRIDESMAIDS

Bridesmaids of the 1950s wore hourglass-shaped dresses. They were usually of a shorter length than the bride's dress, stopping mid-calf.

As with bridal gowns, most bridesmaid's dresses were strapless and worn with a stole, bolero jacket, or other short fitted jacket. For example, a tulle stole would be worn over a strapless dress of embroidered sheer nylon, creating a soft, feminine look.

These dresses were designed for dual purpose. They could be worn for the wedding and then later used as a cocktail dress.

Bridesmaid's Dresses, circa 1955
Photograph, left to right:
Left. *Princess style cotton lace gown with draped Empire bodice of sparkling Crystalette. The dress has a scooped neckline and is worn with a cap sleeve jacket. When the jacket is removed the dress becomes a strapless formal gown.*
Right. *This dress is made of cotton lace and has a long fitted torso. A short sleeved spencer jacket covers the strapless formal underneath.*
Both bridesmaids dresses designed by Beau Time Formals

VINTAGE COLOR PALETTES

IVORY   WHITE   OFF-WHITE

HOW TO USE THE VINTAGE COLOR PALETTES

Most period weddings used color combinations that are not often used or seen anymore. This is both good news and bad. The good news is that almost any combination of the colors in this chapter will make your wedding "look" vintage. The bad news is that since some of the colors are not typical modern-day colors, you might have a hard time finding the shade or color you want. So, I've tried to add enough colors to give you a feel for each era's sense of color. Modern day decorations and fabrics offer tons of colors choices, so even if you can't find the exact period color you want, you can still find a color that resembles it. The basic thing you should remember is this: **The simplest way to make your wedding seem period is to use a pastel or muted color scheme.**

Color definitions have been added for each decade. The color definition will tell you how to mix and combine the colors from each era's color palette. Ivory and off-white boxes have also been added to each color palette. These should be used to compare colors against so you can make color scheme decisions. The color palettes can also be compared to plain white by comparing them to the color of the page.

NOTE: Place a blank sheet of white paper behind the color palette that you're viewing. This will ensure an accurate representation of each decade's color palette.

COLOR SCHEME TIPS & IDEAS

*   **Mix warm shades with other warm shades.** Warm means that the color has an orangy undertone.

*   **Mix cool shades with other cool shades.** Cool means that the color has a bluish undertone.

*   **Decide on one color and then use shades of that color for depth and contrast.** Shades or cream or ivory look very vintage and antique. Or try shades of light blue, with darker blue accents.

*   **Colors schemes that are too dark or muted will look dreary.** Color schemes should be kept on the lighter end.

*   **Combine dark colors with light colors.** This will give you more versatility for decorating.

*   **Use ivory, off white, or a nice creamy white instead of a bright, hospital white.**

1910s PALETTE

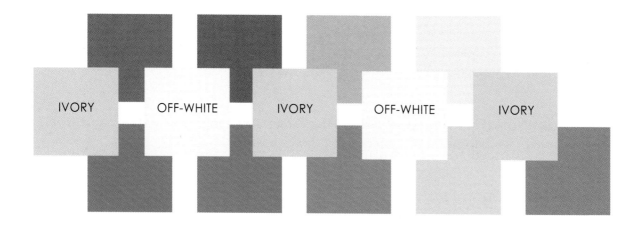

IVORY OFF-WHITE IVORY OFF-WHITE IVORY

1920s PALETTE

MOTIF: MUTED COLORS COMBINED WITH BEIGES AND ROSES.

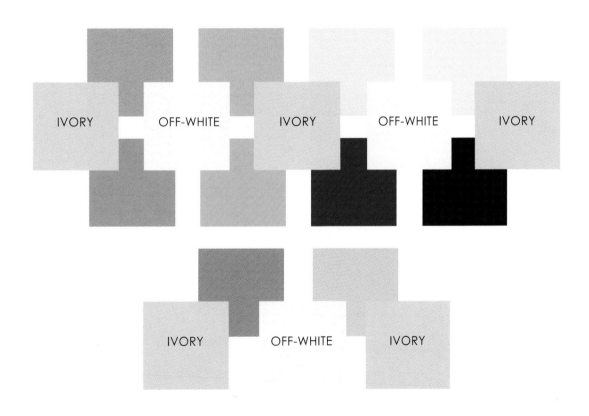

IVORY   OFF-WHITE   IVORY   OFF-WHITE   IVORY

IVORY   OFF-WHITE   IVORY

1930s PALETTE

MOTIF: BRIGHT COLORS COMBINED WITH MUTED COLORS.

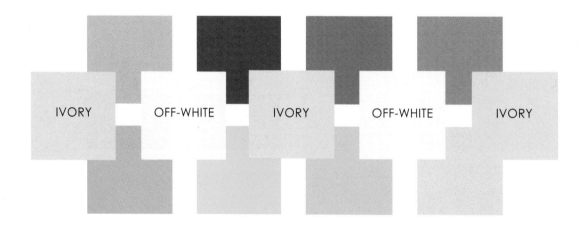

1940s PALETTE

MOTIF: RICH COLORS COMBINED WITH PASTELS.

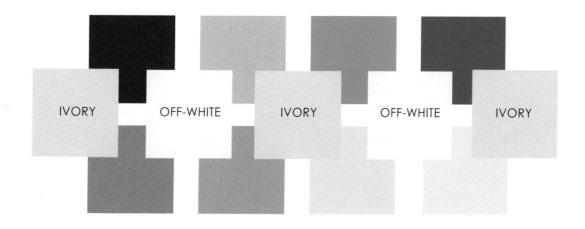

IVORY OFF-WHITE IVORY OFF-WHITE IVORY

1950s PALETTE

MOTIF: EMPHASIS ON PASTELS COMBINED WITH OTHER PASTELS OR RICH COLORS.

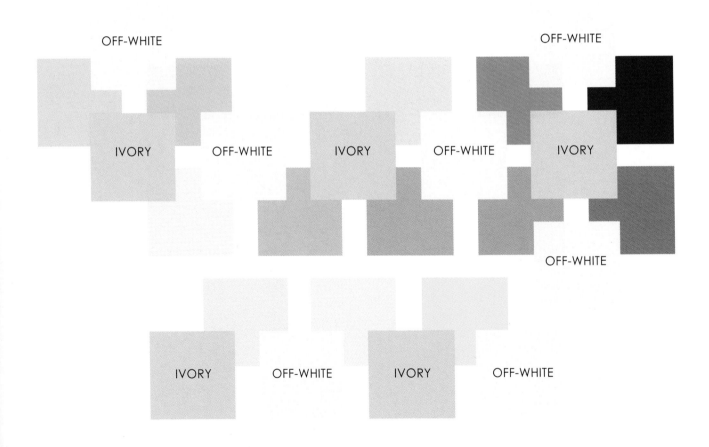

OFF-WHITE

IVORY

OFF-WHITE

OFF-WHITE

IVORY

OFF-WHITE

OFF-WHITE

IVORY

OFF-WHITE

IVORY

OFF-WHITE

IVORY

OFF-WHITE

MEN'S WEAR COLOR PALETTE

MOTIF: TONES OF GRAY, BLUE, AND BLACK.

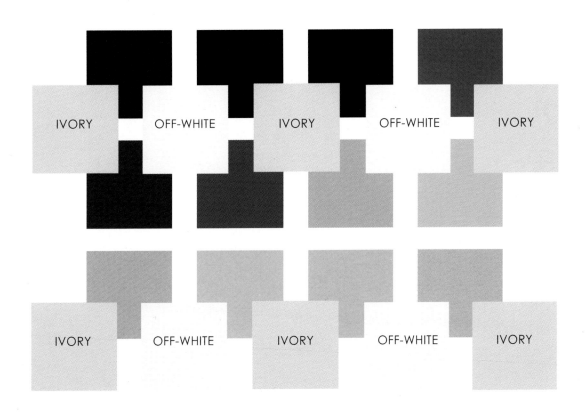

CHAPTER 4
VINTAGE BRIDEGROOM

Men's Wedding Attire
From left to right: White tuxedo coat with black slack for semiformal, summer evening weddings; white tie and black tails for formal evening weddings; black tuxedo and bow tie for semiformal evening weddings; morning coat and striped slacks for formal daytime weddings.

MEN'S VINTAGE ATTIRE

During the first half of the Twentieth Century, men's clothing and costume were strictly determined by the time of day and the formality of the wedding. Modern day wedding attire etiquette has relaxed quite a bit since then, but the clothing worn remains pretty much the same.

BASIC GROOM'S VINTAGE WEDDING ATTIRE:

INFORMAL – Business or Sack Suit.

SEMIFORMAL – Dark Suit or Tuxedo.

FORMAL DAYTIME WEDDINGS – Morning/Cutaway coat. The morning coat tapers down to one tail in the back.

FORMAL EVENING WEDDINGS – Tuxedo or Tailcoat. The tailcoat tapers down to two tails in the back.

Formal men's vintage attire calls for stark contrast. This means that wedding attire should be black and white, ideally black coat and white bow tie. If the bride is in ivory or off white, the groom would then wear black and off white. The exception to the black and white rule is the cutaway coat with striped trousers. In this instance coat, trousers, and accessories make up a combination of gray, black, and white.

Groomsmen typically wear the same outfit as the groom, the only difference would be in the choice of boutonniere. The groom and best man should wear matching boutonnieres, with the groom's being slightly more elaborate. The other groomsmen should wear a different boutonniere from the groom and best man. If it is just the groom and his best man, then the best man should wear a less elaborate boutonniere than the groom.

For vintage looking attire, you can either purchase an original period suit or use the modern day equivalent. More important than finding an original is making sure that any suit you choose fits and looks good. If finding a suit that you like proves difficult, you can always have your period attire custom made. **If going the custom made route *make sure* that you choose an experienced suit maker, and allow plenty of time for the suit to be made.**

SIMPLE GUIDELINES FOR MEN'S FORMAL WEAR

LINE AND STYLING

1910s – High, starched collars, long coats, straight slacks.

1920s – Squarish jacket; straight slacks.

1930s – Jacket with broad, squared shoulders and a slim waist; straight slacks with a high waistline.

1940s – Fitted jacket with slightly broad shoulders; straight slacks with a slightly high waistline.

1950s – Comfortable, fitted jackets with tapered slacks.

SHIRTS

Formal – White, starched shirt with wing collar.

Semiformal – White, starched shirt with turned down collar. *i.e.* A standard dress shirt.

TIE

Ascot - Can be patterned or solid. The pattern should be small and correspond to the color scheme of the wedding.

Four In hand - The pattern should be small and correspond to the color scheme of the wedding.

Bow Tie - Usually black or white. Reserved for formal attire.

VEST - Always wear a vest or cummerbund.

SHOES

Semiformal – Black or two-toned shoes.

Formal – Black, patent leather.

GLOVES
- Gloves of white kid are only worn for formal daytime weddings.

HAT
- Generally not worn for evening weddings.

Informal or Semiformal Daytime – Homburg, fedora, or bowler.

Formal Daytime – Silk top hats.

BOUTONNIERE

Groom - A sample from the bride's bouquet. Typically, lilies of the valley.

Groomsmen - White carnation.

THE 1910s MAN

For the informal daytime wedding, the 1910s man wore a double-breasted sack suit (business suit). The jacket buttoned up high and could be considered equivalent to the modern-day 4-button coat. A vest was worn underneath so as to peak out at the top when the jacket was fully closed. Along with this went a high, stiff wing tip collared shirt (almost grazing the jawbone) and a four-in-hand or white bow tie. The ensemble was then accessorized with a Homburg, bowler, or boater hat (see glossary for definitions), and a straight, tapered cane.

The standard for the formal daytime wedding was the morning coat with gray striped trousers and a silk top hat. The frock coat was an alternative to the morning coat and was popular until WW I. The frock coat was a slightly fitted, square-hemmed jacket that reached almost down to the knees. It was also worn with gray striped trousers and a silk top hat. Illustration is at right (the man, not the woman). Notice that the hemline of the jacket ends at the back of the knees.

The semiformal evening wedding called for a black tuxedo. Formal, evening weddings required the groom to wear black tails with a silk top hat.

Men's Formal Daytime Attire, circa 1914
A long frock coat is worn over gray striped trousers. Accessories include a silk top hat and white kid gloves.

THE 1920s MAN

These were the years of Prohibition and mobsters.
Groom's attire from the 1920s still resembled that of the 1910s. The most noticeable change was that the frock coat was out of fashion.

Since the frock coat was gone, the morning coat became the only standard attire for formal daytime weddings.

For informal daytime weddings, sack suits were still worn with a fedora, boater, Homburg, or bowler hat.

The black tuxedo was still popular for semiformal evening weddings, while black tails and a top hat became the standard for more formal events.

Men's Formal Evening Wear, circa 1928
Black tails and matching slacks worn with a white pique vest, starched wing tip collar, and white bow tie. The ensemble is finished with a white carnation.

THE 1930s MAN

During the 1930s, formality in clothing was a little less strict than in previous decades. The sack suit turned into the business suit and the morning coat was worn less often.

"A bridegroom who wants to depart from the conventional cutaway coat with striped trousers and silk hat will find this navy blue double breasted sack suit an excellent choice and in perfectly good taste. The wing collar with small patterned black and white bow tie, a white carnation in the buttonhole and black shoes give the formal accessory notes." circa 1930.

Another departure from the traditional morning coat was the wearing of an oxford gray jacket with gray striped trousers. Jacket is shown at left. Black shoes, wing collar, black and white tie, and derby hat were the standard accessories.

A variation for formal summer daytime weddings was to combine white flannel trousers the oxford gray jacket.

Formal evening weddings still required grooms to wear black tails.

Men's Suit, circa 1930
A double breasted jacket is worn with high waisted slacks. A starched white shirt is worn with a wing tip collar and black bow tie for a more formal look. The ensemble is accessorized with a white linen handkerchief in the breast pocket and a carnation boutonniere.

THE 1940s MAN

Many men joined the service during the war, which lasted until 1945. Weddings were done at the last minute often on base before shipping out. Formal weddings were definitely not the norm. Wedding attire conventions for the 1940s man were relaxed and modified to suit the situation.

The 1940s man wore the single or double-breasted business suit with a fedora, homburg, or straw hat. This was appropriate attire for the informal daytime wedding. If he was an enlisted man, his service uniform would be worn.

Civilian men wore morning coats for formal daytime weddings. A formal wedding for the enlisted man required full dress uniform.

Evening weddings required a tuxedo jacket or black tails.

Man in Uniform, circa 1943
Bridegroom is in dress uniform.

THE 1950s MAN

Following the trend of relaxing wedding conventions, the 1950s man had more choices regarding what type of wedding attire to wear.

A business suit worn with a gray felt hat was preferred for informal daytime weddings, while a bluish gray jacket worn with white flannel slacks was typical for garden weddings.

A groom's options for the formal daytime wedding were to wear either the traditional morning coat or an all white suit. The all white suit would be accessorized with a straw fedora.

Evening weddings called for either a black or midnight blue tuxedo. At night, midnight blue looks blacker than black.

Another popular variation was the white dinner jacket worn with midnight blue dress trousers. Tails, only this time in navy blue, were worn for very formal events.

Informal Summer Wedding Attire, circa 1954
A midnight blue jacket is worn with flannel slacks and white buckskin shoes. The shirt is white with a fold down collar and is worn with a white four in hand tie.

MORNING COAT AND ACCESSORIES

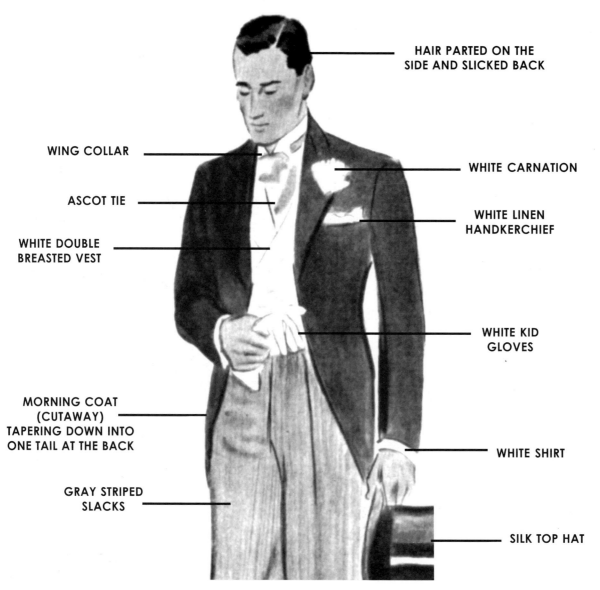

HAIR PARTED ON THE SIDE AND SLICKED BACK

WING COLLAR

ASCOT TIE

WHITE DOUBLE BREASTED VEST

WHITE CARNATION

WHITE LINEN HANDKERCHIEF

WHITE KID GLOVES

MORNING COAT (CUTAWAY) TAPERING DOWN INTO ONE TAIL AT THE BACK

WHITE SHIRT

GRAY STRIPED SLACKS

SILK TOP HAT

TAILCOAT AND ACCESSORIES

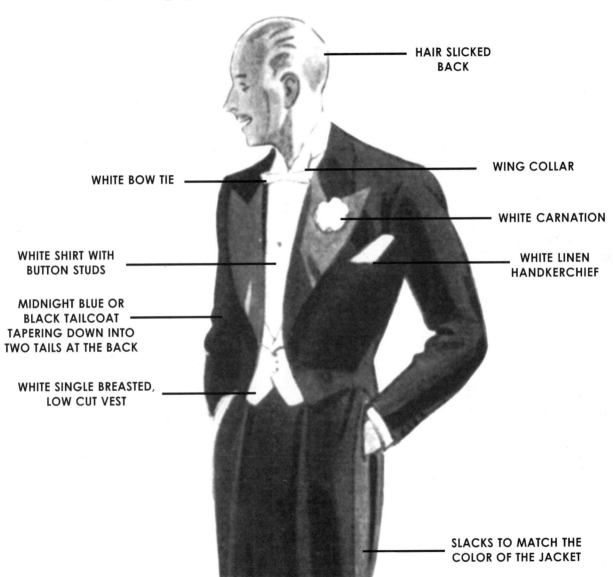

HAIR SLICKED BACK

WING COLLAR

WHITE BOW TIE

WHITE CARNATION

WHITE SHIRT WITH BUTTON STUDS

WHITE LINEN HANDKERCHIEF

MIDNIGHT BLUE OR BLACK TAILCOAT TAPERING DOWN INTO TWO TAILS AT THE BACK

WHITE SINGLE BREASTED, LOW CUT VEST

SLACKS TO MATCH THE COLOR OF THE JACKET

MEN'S ACCESSORIES & VARIOUS TIPS

SHOES

WING TIP SHOE
Worn in the 20s, 30s, and 40s.

COMMON DRESS SHOE
Worn in the 10s, 20s, 30s, 40s and 50s.

STRAIGHT-TIPPED BAL/CAP TOE
Worn in the 10s, 20s, 30s, and 40s.

TIP #1: TYING AN ASCOT

Follow the steps in numbered order.

METHOD 1

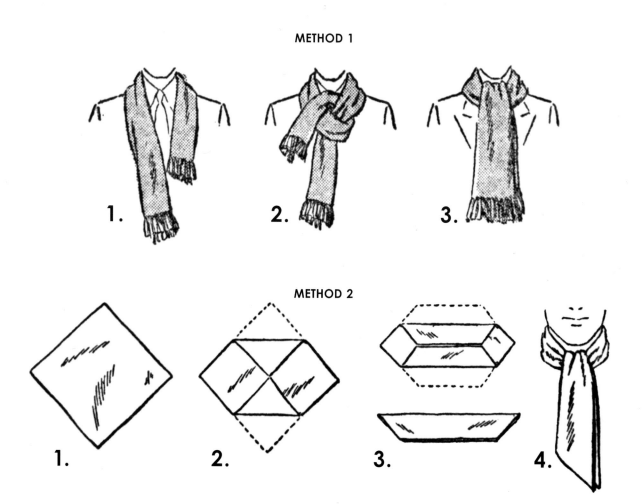

METHOD 2

TIP #2: TYING THE FOUR-IN-HAND

TIP #3: TYING THE WINDSOR KNOT

TIP #4: TYING THE BOW TIE

TIP #5: FOLDING A HANDKERCHIEF

The handkerchief should be linen. Once it has been folded, place it in the left breast pocket with the corners pointing upward.

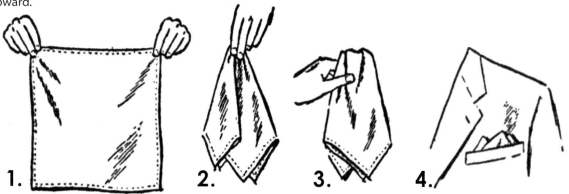

TIP #6: KEEPING YOUR SHIRT STRAIGHT

From left to right: your dress shirt can be safety-pinned to your pants; safety-pinned to your suspenders; tucked into your underwear.

CHAPTER 5
VINTAGE WEDDING & RECEPTION

VENUE/LOCATION CHOICES

Vintage weddings and receptions can take place anywhere from a backyard garden to the most formal of churches and reception halls. How you decorate your location and what type of music you play will contribute to the vintage feel of your wedding. The most common locations that lend themselves to period weddings include historic ballrooms, historic hotels, old-style restaurants, lush gardens, and historic homes or mansions. Most cities have a variety of these types of venues (you'll find a brief national listing of such places in the back of this book). Many of the historic venues in your city may not be advertised or normally rentable. So, if you've fallen in love with a place, see if they'll rent it out to you – there's no harm in asking.

When shopping around for a venue, take note of how your contact person treats you and addresses your concerns. More than likely, your guests will be treated the same way. You should also follow your gut instincts. If your contact person at the location fails to give you any straight answers, be wary. There have been numerous horror stories about fabulous locations that turned out to be nightmares because the management failed to notify the bride and groom of specific regulations regarding the facilities. **Make sure that you get everything in writing**. Remember, service contracts are generally written by the service provider, with their own protection in mind.

No matter how wonderful the location is, being comfortable with the location and its staff is most important. They will single-handedly be responsible for how smoothly your wedding runs.

VINTAGE DECORATING

Wedding decorations during the first half of the Twentieth Century were all pretty similar. The main decorating differences between the decades were the color palettes used. (Please refer to the vintage color palettes chapter starting back on page 91.). Most weddings were decorated with flowers, candles and tulle. See page 73 for a list of flowers typically used in vintage weddings.

The goal in decorating for a vintage wedding is to create a vintage atmosphere that makes your guests feel as if they've stepped back into another era – without having it seem silly or gauche. Decorating your location for your period wedding is easy if you remember one basic rule: **Less is more.**

LESS IS MORE

The "less is more" attitude is very important. This does not mean you cut out all creativity and color. It just means that you should keep things simple and clean looking. A small amount of beautiful flowers placed nicely is much more subtle and elegant than a huge amount of flowers that are overtaking the room.

CREATING AMBIANCE

Ambiance is one of the most important keys to creating a vintage atmosphere. Choosing a historic location makes this very easy. If you're getting married in a historic or period building, chances are the ambiance is already there. Decorations would then be used to enhance it and make it comfortable for you and your guests. If you are not getting married in a historical location, you may have to create the ambiance from scratch.

Ambiance can be mostly enhanced or created by combining simple decorations with a vintage color scheme. Decorating can be done with a variety of things including plants, fabric, candlelight, and lamps. *How* you use the decorations for your venue is what will create the vintage look and feel of your wedding.

DECORATING TIPS

TIP # 1 - USE A PASTEL OR MUTED COLOR SCHEME

Creating a vintage atmosphere is easy when you use vintage colors to decorate. Pastel and muted shades lend themselves nicely to historic venues. They also tend to create an antique look which will help in the overall vintage atmosphere you're trying to create. Pastels and muted colors should be combined with ivory, off-white, or cream. Combining colors with a bright white should be avoided if possible. For more explanation on choosing colors please refer to the vintage color palettes section starting back on page 91.

TIP #2 - USE CANDLELIGHT

Weddings of the first half of the Twentieth Century used candles extensively for evening weddings. They are a classic decorating tool that can be used very effectively in creating a romantic vintage feel for your wedding. They are by far the most versatile decorating tool that you can use for an evening event. What could be more beautiful than being married by candlelight?

If you are working with a small budget, wonders can be done with candlelight. Candlelight as a main decorating tool works most effectively in smaller settings. Pillars of ivory or cream colored candles generally look best in trying to create a vintage feel. White candles tend to be too bright and less subtle. Pastels may also work if the color is faint. Stay away from intensely colored candles as they tend not to glow. Also make sure to use unscented candles. This is the only surefire way not bother any of your guests with overpowering scents.

If you're using candles as your *main* decorating tool, you should use tons of them everywhere. Small tea lights left in little nooks and alcoves creates a wonderful romantic atmosphere. Very tall candles covered with hurricane lamps can be set along walkways for a romantically lit pathway. Make sure however, that they are off to the side and out of range from foot traffic. Candles set in the restrooms and hallways are a personal touch that everyone enjoys.

Candles can also be used as centerpieces for the tables. A bundle of three or four pillars (or more depending on how large the table is) can be arranged in the center of each table. They can be left as is, or surrounded with white flowers such as lilies of the valley, orange blossoms, or Queen Anne's lace. Make sure that the candles are not too high, as people will want to talk and see each other across the table. Many venues will require that you have the candles in containers to control the open flame. In this case, candles can be left in clear glass containers.

Another decorating idea comes from the 1930s. For an evening garden reception, place dozens of candles set into little squat glasses in the center of every table, and hang plain white, candle-lit, Japanese lanterns from the tree tops around the garden.

TIP # 4 - DECORATE WITH VINTAGE PLANTS AND FLOWER ARRANGEMENTS
(see page 73 for a complete list of vintage flowers and plants)
Plants and flowers are used to add color, beauty, and texture to your setting. They can also be used to hide problem areas or impart an entirely different look to your location. Using plants and foliage will help you a great deal if you need to create ambiance from scratch.

WHITE FLOWERS WITH GREENERY
Flowers make beautiful accents and are generally used to decorate tables, walkways, and wedding altars. During the first half of the Twentieth Century, the basic look for flower arrangements consisted of white flowers surrounded by greenery and candles. Fern, evergreen boughs, or ivy were popular for greenery, while orange blossoms, lilies of the valley, and roses were standard flower choices.

Flowers make great centerpieces. For long dining tables, try single stems of larkspur, lupine, foxglove or Canterbury bells, placed in single small vases down the length of the table. This decorating idea originally came from 1935, but has a very modern simple feel to it. A low arrangement of sweet peas, lilies of the valley and primroses packed tightly into small glass vases or jars can also make a sweet centerpiece.

Buffet tables can also be decorated quite beautifully to look vintage. Simply decorate the tables with greenery like evergreen boughs and fern. Or, place a long row of jelly jars down the center of the table. The jars should be rim to rim and packed full of flowers, such as white phlox and Queen Anne's Lace. Hide the jars with moss or other greenery.

Large flowers should be used as decorative ornaments. Large white phlox plants (or any other large white flowering plant) can be placed into enormous pots and set along the bridal path to create an elegant walkway. Fern or moss can be tucked into the tops of the planters to hide stems and to create a more uniform look. Tall graceful sprays of Queen Anne's lace, arranged with plenty of green, makes for an interesting ceremony backdrop. Queen Anne's lace can also be used to fill large glass vases and set on windowsills or the floor.

PLANTS, TREES, AND FOLIAGE

Foliage and plants come in a variety of sizes and shapes and can be used to completely redo a room. You can usually find greens in larger quantities and they also tend to cost less than flowers. Because of this, shrubs, vines, and ferns were used extensively during the first half of the Twentieth Century to decorate wedding and reception halls. Lots of decorating could be done without lots of money.

Plants that were most often used include: mountain laurel, which has pink flowers and glossy green leaves; wild climbing roses combined with wild clematis vines and ferns from the woods; banks of black-eyed Susan combined with outdoor ferns, bowers of snowy dogwood in season and fluffy wild pink azalea; decorative spring and early summer shrubs; and cherry blossom branches.

Plants, trees, and foliage can be used to distinguish sections of importance. For example, a decorating tip used for a daytime garden wedding from the 1930s calls for an arbor of chicken wire woven with evergreen boughs. This arbor creates a gazebo area for cake cutting. It looks divinely cool, and it smells like the deep woods. Twinkle lights can be woven in with the evergreen boughs for an evening reception.

If you need to completely transform a room (as in the case of a large, plain reception hall), a fair amount of tropical foliage and plants, such as palm trees, can be placed around the room. Using them will impart a 1940s dinner theater or a 1950s tropical tiki room effect.

TIP #5 - USE IVORY OR CREAM COLORED TABLE LINENS

A vintage style wedding calls for white, ivory, or cream table linens (whichever matches best with your color scheme) . You should use flowers, favors, and decorations to provide any color that you may want to bring to the table.

White linens are beautiful, but they are often too bright and can be glaring. Ivory or off-white linens will still impart a "white linen" effect, but look much more vintage. Another option is to use lace tablecloths. These tend to look more antique than white linens, and will still match well with a pastel or muted color scheme.

TIP #6 - USE FABRIC SPARSELY

Tulle and gauze were used during the first half of the Twentieth Century, but not as extensively as they are used in modern day weddings. Weddings from the first half of the Twentieth Century relied much more on greenery and plants for decorations. Tulle and gauze were mainly used as accent pieces for favors and aisle decorations at church weddings. If you really have your heart set on soft billowy gauze or tulle for decorating, be sure to follow the "less is more" rule. Draped gauze, tulle, or other sheer fabrics can add drama and elegance to doorways, table linens, and chair covers.

TIP #7 - USE PLACE CARDS

If you'd like a specific seating arrangement for the reception, place cards are necessary. The place cards should be off-white, ivory, or cream color. The writing should be hand scripted or printed in a vintage-looking type face. You can also decorate the place cards to give them a little vintage flare. This can be done by attaching ribbons, lace, or flowers. See example at right.

VINTAGE FAVORS

Giving wedding favors is one of most personal ways that you can thank your guests for their attendance and their help in celebrating your special day. Wedding favors not only let your guests know that you are thankful, but can also help add a vintage touch to your reception. Favors can either be store bought and decorated or else made at home. Here are some tips and ideas that will help get you started.

TIP #1 - LET THEM EAT CAKE...AND THEN SOME...

Cake boxes were the standard favor given at weddings throughout the first half of the Twentieth Century. Pre-sliced wedding cake or individual mini wedding cakes were placed into decorative boxes for the guests to take home. The boxes were inscribed with the initials of the newlyweds and trimmed with ribbon and flowers. Plain white cake boxes can still be found today, but you'll most likely have to decorate them yourself. Two examples of period cake boxes are shown at right.

TIP #2 - MAKE IT LOOK VINTAGE

It almost goes without saying that the packaging is most important, especially when trying to create a vintage look for the favors. It almost doesn't matter what goes into the packaging as long as it looks nice. Jars, tins, and fabric bags all lend themselves to easy decorating ideas. Antique jars and tins are preferable and can be found at antique stores and thrift shops. If you are planning on using real antique or vintage packaging, don't worry if they are mismatched. They should, however, have in common at least one of the aspects, listed below:

- All are the same color or shades of the same color; *i.e.* shades of light blue and aquamarine.
- All are the same type of shape and size; *i.e.* small round jars of the same shape but with different textures.
- All have a common theme or message; *i.e.* love, marriage, wedding.

TIP #3 - PERSONALIZE CARDS

A small card with a personal message also adds a very nice touch. Small cards can be attached to the favors with a recipe, message, or simply the guest's name written on it. If you decide to add the guest's name to the card, the favor can then double as the place card for seating arrangements. The writing should be hand scripted or printed in a vintage style type face (see page 150 for type face examples).

OTHER IDEAS FOR FAVORS

- A glass jar filled with white chocolate can be trimmed with ivory satin ribbon and wax orange blossoms for a decidedly 1920s look.

- Roses are synonymous with romance and can be used as favors that add an antique romantic feel to the table. Fresh or dried rose petals can be placed in antique tins or jars and dressed with ribbon. Attach a small card with recipes of what to do with them. For example: Dried petals can be used in the bath for a luxurious sent, while fresh petals can be eaten with gourmet meals.

- Other beautiful flowers and fragrant herbs can also be given as favors. Bundle up your favorite herbs or flowers with ribbon or antique lace for a vintage look . Orange blossoms, lily of the valley, or fragrant lavender can be tied with satin ribbon and given as gifts at the simple garden wedding. Dried herb and teas can be packaged into antique tins, jars, or muslin bags and trimmed with a handwritten recipe card and ribbon.

VINTAGE PROGRAMS

Printed or hand-scripted programs are a vintage touch that are not commonly found in modern weddings. Programs are a wonderful way to welcome guests and provide useful information for the wedding ceremony. Normally the ceremony order, the name of the officiant, songs to be played during the ceremony, and bridal party names are enclosed within a program. Most wedding invitation dealers can also create your wedding program. Below is an example of one way a program may be worded.

Wedding of
Martha and Raymond Chandler
September 2, 2001
Ebell Club

Prelude	*Prelude in F Major*	*Matron of honor*	*Francis Bennett*
		Attendants	*Lucille Freis*
Processional	*Bridal Chorus*		*Betty Gershon*
Invocation		*Best Man*	*Raymond Scott*
		Groomsmen	*Charles Silter*
Exchange of the Vows			*Anthony Gray*
Recessional	*Wedding March*	*Flower Girl*	*Dottie Fray*
		Ring Bearer	*Bobby Smith*

VINTAGE CAKES

Here's everything you need to know about the kinds of wedding cakes served during the first half of the Twentieth Century.

THE WEDDING CAKE

This is a dark fruitcake made with brandy or rum covered with light frosting, decorations, and real flowers.

THE BRIDE'S CAKE

This is a light, white cake covered with white frosting and decorations. There would be a small glass ring or trinket baked into the cake. When sliced, whoever found the trinket or ring in their piece was the next to be married.

THE GROOM'S CAKE

This is a dark fruitcake made with brandy or rum and covered with a dark frosting.

Most cake that was served at weddings would be served in slices or as small individual cakes for each guest. Small individual cakes were decorated with the bride and groom's initials and frosted in pastel colors. Mini cakes would either be round or molded into shapes. Popular shapes included hearts, wedding bells, cupids, bride-figure, groom-figure, four leaf clover, slipper, horseshoes, calla lilies, or lilies of the valley.

Normally, the bride's cake would be cut and served at the reception and the groom's cake or wedding cake would be pre-cut and placed into cake boxes as favors for the guests to take home. If the traditional wedding cake was to be served at the reception, pre-cut slices would still be placed in cake boxes as favors for the guests to take home.

The tradition of the bride's cake has been kept through the years, but is now made without the trinkets. The old fashioned bride's cake is what we call "wedding cake" at a modern reception. The traditional wedding cake of brandy and fruit seems to have disappeared along with the tradition of cake boxes as favors. However, the tradition of the groom's cake seems to have been kept alive in the South and is served at the reception along with a light bride's cake.

VINTAGE CAKE DECORATIONS

CAKE TOPPERS

If you want to extend the look of your vintage wedding to your cake decorations, vintage cake toppers are the way to do it. Vintage cake toppers from the early Twentieth Century were very elaborate. They usually consisted of a bride and groom figurine, but could sometimes incorporate figurines of the entire bridal party. Period cake toppers usually have the bride and groom figurines dressed in period attire. This looks very cute, especially if you and the groom are dressed the same way as the cake topper figurines.

Most vintage cake toppers are made of wax, ceramic, or chalk-ware and would often have clothing of fabric or paper. Many of these cake toppers have been saved through the years and are somewhat easily available. You can check auction listings on ebay or a reputable antique source.

FLOWERS

Many period cakes were decorated with fresh or paste orange blossoms and lilies of the valley. Paste blossoms can be easily created by an experienced cake maker, while your florist can provide you with fresh orange blossoms and lilies of the valley to be placed on and around the cake.

Another way to decorate your cake with flowers is to have your cake maker place a vase in the center of the cake. Flowers can then be placed in the vase. This was also very popular to do during the early Twentieth Century. See example at right.

Wedding Cake, circa 1937
The photograph is of a three tiered wedding cake. It is frosted white with little rosettes around the sides. A vase is placed in the center of the cake and filled with lilies of the valley.

VINTAGE CAKE RECIPES

BRIDE'S CAKE , CIRCA 1913
Cream one half cupful of butter and add gradually, while beating constantly, one and one-half cupfuls of fine granulated sugar; then add one-half cupful milk alternately with two one-half cupfuls of flour mixed and sifted with three teaspoonfuls of baking powder and one fourth teaspoonful of cream of tartar. Beat whites of six eggs until stiff and add to first mixture. Flavor with one-half teaspoonful of almond extract. Bake in a moderate oven.
Cover with *White Mountain Cream Frosting. Decorate with ornamental frosting, or not, as you like.

*WHITE MOUNTAIN CREAM FROSTING, CIRCA 1913
Put one cupful of sugar and one-third cupful of boiling water in a saucepan and stir to prevent sugar from adhering to pan. Bring to boiling point and boil with as little stirring as possible until syrup will spin a thread when dropped from the tip of a spoon. Pour syrup gradually, while beating constantly, on the whites of two eggs (beaten until stiff but not dry), and continue the beating, until the mixture is of the right consistency to spread. Flavor with almond extract, pour over cake and spread evenly, using the back of a spoon.

BRIDE'S CAKE, CIRCA 1925

1 ⅛ cup butter	¾ teaspoon soda
2 ¼ cups sugar	¾ cup milk
3 ½ cups pastry flour	12 egg whites
2 ¼ teaspoons cream of tartar	1 teaspoon almond extract

Cream the butter and add gradually one cup sugar. Sift pastry flour, measure three and one-half cups and sift again with cream of tartar and soda. Add alternately with milk to first mixture and beat until very light and smooth. Beat egg whites until light and add remaining sugar gradually. Fold into first mixture with the extract. Bake in two pans of the same shape but one smaller than the other for forty to fifty minutes in a moderate oven or at 350 F. Put together with the smaller cake on top, frost and decorate, garnishing with flowers and asparagus fern.

TRADITIONAL WEDDING CAKE, CIRCA 1941

All-purpose flour, sifted, 5 cups
Cinnamon, 2 teaspoons
Allspice, 4 teaspoons
Mace, ¾ teaspoon
Nutmeg, ½ teaspoon
Raisins, seeded, 1 pound
Currants, 1 pound
Candied lemon peel, ½ pound
Candied orange peel, ½ pound
Candied cherries, 1 ½ pounds
Strawberry jam or preserves, 1 pint

Candied pineapple, 1 ½ pounds
Almonds, blanched and shredded, 1 pound
Pecan meats, chopped, 1 pound
Shortening, 1 pound
Orange or pineapple juice, ½ cup
Brown sugar, light, 1 pound
Eggs, separated, 12
Molasses, light, 1 cup
Brandy or cider, ½ cup
Candied citron, 1 ½ pounds

1. Sift flour, measure, add baking soda, spices.
2. Add prepared fruits and nuts and mix.
3. Cream shortening, add sugar gradually; cream together until light and fluffy.
4. Add well-beaten egg yolks, molasses and strawberries.
5. Add liquids (brandy or cider and juices).
6. Add flour and fruit mixture and mix until well blended.
7. Fold in stiffly beaten egg whites.
8. Turn into greased pans lined with waxed paper. (Batter should fill ¾ -full 3 round pans of 6, 8, and 10 inch diameter, 3 inches deep.) Use pans with solid bottoms or spring form pans with tight closures. Cover tops of pans with heavy waxed or parchment paper, fasten well with string; then steam and bake as follows:
9. Steam 6-inch pan 2 ½ hours; 8-inch pan 3 hours; 10-inch pan 3 ½ hours; using any utensil that cake pans will fit into without resting directly in water; for example a rack placed in a clothes boiler, preserving kettle, or double roasting pan. Keep heat very low but steady so that there will be a constant supply of steam.
10. Remove covers and bake all sizes for 1 ½ hours in slow oven (250 F.).
    Note: If an all-baking method is desired, cover as for steaming, during all but the last hour of the baking period; 4 hours for 6-inch pans, 4 ½ hours for 8-inch pans and 5 hours for 10-inch pans. All baking makes for a drier cake than part steaming.

This recipe makes 15 pounds of cake.

Fruitcake should be made several weeks before the wedding; it improves on standing. Keep it in an airtight container, then a day or two before the wedding frost and decorate it. Frost the top and sides of each layer with any glossy white frosting. Frost each layer as you put it in place. Let this stand until it is good and firm, and then decorate it with pearl frosting. **Recipe given on the next page.**

PEARL FROSTING FOR WEDDING CAKE, CIRCA 1941

Beat 2 egg whites until stiff; add 1 cup confectioners' sugar and beat until smooth and thick. Cream ¼ cup vegetable shortening; add ½ cup confectioners' sugar and mix until well blended. Combine these two mixtures; add 1 teaspoon glycerin (optional) and ½ teaspoon almond extract. (The glycerin helps keep the frosting glossy and soft) Gradually add about ½ cup more confectioners' sugar until frosting will hold its shape, beating constantly. Use to decorate cake, which has already been frosted with white frosting as described on the previous page.

WEDDING CAKE, CIRCA 1955

Serves 60 guests

1 lb castor sugar	1 lb plain flour
1 lb butter	1 good pinch of salt
8 eggs	1 level teaspoon mixed spice
1 lb seedless raisins	½ level teaspoon nutmeg
1 lb sultanas	juice and grated rind of lemon
12 oz. currants	3 tablespoonfuls sherry, brandy, or rum
4 oz. seedless raisins	1 tablespoon molasses
4 oz. chopped glace cherries	4 oz. chopped toasted almonds
4 oz. chopped mixed fruit peel	

A well-scrubbed hand is the best mixing utensil. But be sure that everything is prepared and measured out before hand. Wash and prepare the fruit one day, mix the second day, bake the third day.

Use a very deep 9-inch (7 pound) baking tin. Line with well-greased brown paper. Pour cake batter in. Place the cake below the center of the oven and cook for an hour at 315 F, and for another 4 ½ hours at 250 F. The true test to see if the cake is done is by plunging a metal skewer or knitting needle into the center. If it comes out clean, the cake is finished. If the cake is browning too quickly, put some brown paper or aluminum foil over the top…and don't forget to make a hollow in the mixture, ½ inch deep, to give the risen cake a flat surface.

When the baked cake has cooled 10 minutes, ease it out of the tin, and allow to cool completely. Then either:
(a) Make skewer holes over the bottom and pour over a further 2 tablespoonfuls of spirit; wrap in greaseproof paper and store in an airtight tin OR (b) Saturate some cheesecloth with cooking sherry, wrap around the cake, then cover with aluminum foil and store in a dust-proof, dry cupboard.

Have the icing done professionally.

BASIC CAKE TERMS

BUTTERCREAM FROSTING: An off white or ivory colored soft frosting with a butter base.

FONDANT: Rolled out to a uniform thickness and carefully fitted over the specially prepared tiers. Looks very smooth.

GUM PASTE: Used to form lovely flowers and other decorations.

LAYERS: Individual slabs of cake that are assembled together to form a tier.

MARZIPAN: This is colored almond paste. Marzipan looks fabulous for colorful cake decorations and figurines.

ROYAL ICING: An egg white based icing that becomes plaster hard.

SEPARATORS: The "legs" that are sometimes used to elevate one tier above the other.

SUGAR PASTE: Used for covering cakes and for modelling flowers or sculptures.

TIER: Used together to form the finished cake.

VINTAGE RECEPTION MENUS

The unwritten rule is that if you've invited people to your reception, they're expecting some sort of sustenance in the way of food and drink. The layout does not have to be dramatic or opulent, but everyone should be able to get a little something to eat and drink regardless whether your party is formal or not.

Three types of menus were commonly used in the early half of the Twentieth Century. The two simplest menus, were to serve either punch and sandwiches or coffee and cake. This was fine for a crowd and suitable for any time except an actual meal hour. For a meal hour reception, a salad would be added in with the sandwiches and served with both coffee and punch. This was adequate for lunch or supper and was also suitable for an evening wedding.

Many of the period food preparations and menus will seem strange as you read them, and have really just been included for an interesting read. If you decide to serve something from a period menu, make sure that you or your caterer tries out the recipe first to make sure that your guests will not be frightened away by the sight or taste of it. Included here are both simple and elaborate reception menus that were used for wedding breakfasts (meal served to the guests after a morning wedding), buffets, and sit down dinners.

1910s

MENU I

Belmont chicken, lettuce sandwiches
Molded salmon, reception rolls
Praline ring, strawberry ice cream
Lady fingers
Macaroons
Bride's cake

MENU II

Shrimps a la Bechamel
Bread and butter folds
Ham mousse, cream fingers
Strawberry bombe, pound cake
Sultana sticks
Salted almonds
Wedding cake in boxes

MENU III

Iced consomme
Lobster salad
Jellied meats, chicken pates
Sandwiches, finger rolls
Ices
Cake

1920s

MENU I

Chestnut Puree
Chicken a la King
Cheese straw or cheese fingers
Melba Toast
Frozen pudding
Cake

MENU II

Canapés (caviar, pate de foi gras, anchovy,
lobster, sardine)
Cold boneless chicken in aspic
Alligator pear salad
Small buttered finger rolls
Cake

1930s

MENU I

Ginger fruit cocktail
Lobster cardinal in patty cases
Watercress sandwiches
Chicken and ham mousse in aspic
Lover's knot rolls
Bride's cake
Orange flower bisque in
chocolate boxes

MENU II

Turkey and veal salad
Cold sliced Virginia ham
Bread and butter sandwiches
Hot Boston baked beans
Ice cream
Wedding Cake
Doughnuts

MENU III

Ham and veal loaf
Bride's salad
Salad greens
Honey cream dressing
Cheese rolls
Fancy sandwiches
Ice cream
Bride's cake
Almond cookies

1940s & 1950s

MENU I

Salted nuts, cheese biscuits
Cream cheese dip
Potato crisps, cocktail onions
Sherried mushroom soup
Boiled salmon in lettuce cups,
Potato salad
String bean relish
French rolls and butter
Lemon refrigerator cakes
Strawberry meringues

MENU II

Chicken salads
Fancy sandwiches
Ice cream
Small cakes
Coffee, punch
Nuts, mints, bonbons

MENU III

Assorted bridge rolls.
Pinwheel and checkerboard
sandwiches
Bite-size sausage rolls
Savory cheese tartlets
Miniature fish cakes
Brandy snaps
Bridal petits fours
Individual sherry charlotte russe
Brandied fruit salad and ice cream

MENU RECIPES

STRAWBERRY BOMBE, CIRCA 1913

Caramelize one-half cupful of sugar, add one-half cupful of chopped blanched filberts, turn into a buttered pan, cool, then pound in mortar and put through a puree strainer. Beat the yolks of four eggs until thick, add gradually three-fourths cupful of hot caramel syrup, and cook in double boiler until mixture thickens, then beat until cold. Fold in one and one-third cupfuls of heavy cream, beaten until stiff. Then add prepared nut meats, one-half teaspoonful of vanilla and a few grains of salt. Line melon mold with strawberry ice, turn in mixture, pack in rock salt and finely crushed ice, using one part of salt to two parts of ice, and let stand three hours.
Editors Note: Packing the concoction in salt and ice is the same as freezing it. It's probably easier to put it in the freezer.

THE BRIDE'S SALAD, CIRCA 1937

Cut off bottom of honeydew melon so that the melon will stand. Scoop balls from inside with French vegetable cutter; reserve balls to use in salad. Wind white satin baby ribbon all around upper part of small china doll. Secure veil on head with ribbon and a few stitches; leave a long train. Around head place a few tiny white flowers. Cut small hole in top of scooped out melon and slip in the doll up to waist. Make a bouquet; place in doll's right arm. Place bride on outer edge of large round platter, allowing the train to lie outside the platter. In front of the bride make a heart of halved strawberries, surrounded by melon balls. Garnish with grapes. Around edge of platter arrange a border of chicory.

BRIDAL PETITS FOURS, CIRCA 1954

Bake a sponge or sandwich mixture in a 12 by 8 cake tin. When cold, cut in rectangles, squares and triangles. Coat in pale tints of glace icing – lemon, pink, violet, white – and decorate daintily with crystallized violets, rose petals, mimosa balls, angelica and cherries. Put in fancy paper cases.
Will keep for several days.

INDIVIDUAL LEMON REFRIGERATOR CAKES, CIRCA 1954

With small cases this serves 16-20 Guests.
Line the bottom of 12 individual sundae glasses or waxed trifle cases with a round of sponge cake. Beat 4 egg yolks until thick. Add ½ cup of lemon juice and 1 dessert spoonful of rind, with ½ lb of sugar, stir well. Soak 1 level dessert spoonful of gelatin in 4 tablespoonfuls of cold water for 5 minutes. Then dissolve the gelatin over hot water – place bowl over kettle – and stir into yolk mixture. Fold in the 4 egg whites, beaten until they hold stiff peaks, and ¾ pint evaporated milk or cream, whipped stiff. Chill the mixture till it's beginning to set, then pour into individual dishes, and leave to set. Decorate with glace cherries and angelica. A little cream may be omitted from the mixture and used as decoration.

BEVERAGES

Typically throughout the early Twentieth Century, beverages like ice water, fruit punch, and coffee were staple offerings at any reception. Champagne was served for the toast throughout the early decades.

During prohibition (1919-1929), alcohol was outlawed and punch had to suffice. A 1920s reception always offered the choice between a hot and a cold drink. Instead, hot drinks like coffee, tea, or hot chocolate were kept in electric metal urns on either ends of the buffet table. Cold drinks like iced tea, iced coffee, chocolate milk, lemonade, orangeade, limeade, fruit lemonade or another kind of fruit punch was served in a large bowl with ladle and surrounded by handled punch glasses. Punch bases most often used were iced tea, ginger ale (white or dark), or grape juice (white or dark).

FRUIT PUNCH RECIPE, CIRCA 1913
Make a syrup by boiling one cupful of water and two cupfuls of sugar for ten minutes. Add one cupful of tea infusion, two cupfuls of strawberry syrup, juice of five lemons, juice of five oranges and one can of grated pineapple. Cover and let stand thirty minutes. Strain and add ice water to make one and one-half gallons of liquid. Add one quart of Apolinaris and one cupful maraschino cherries. Serve in a punch bowl with a large piece of ice. This quantity is sufficient to allow for fifty guests.

PUNCH COMBINATIONS, CIRCA 1920s
White grape juice and ginger ale.
Orange juice and ginger ale.
Garnish the punch with mint leaves and slices of orange and lemon.

SPARKLING PUNCH, CIRCA 1952
Serves 25 Guests
Into the largest basin you've got, pour ½ bottle each of orange and pineapple cordial, ¼ bottle of lime juice, 1 tablespoonful Angostura bitters, ½ teacup of gin, and 1 liqueur glass or miniature bottle of any chosen liqueur. Just before serving, dilute to taste with 4 large bottles of lemonade, and garnish with slices of orange, lemon, cucumber, and seedless grapes.

VINTAGE COCKTAILS

A fun alternative or addition to the basic bar at a reception are period cocktails. Names of the cocktails and years that they were popular can be printed on menus and left at the bar or on reception programs. This not only adds to the idea of a vintage wedding, but offers guests a chance to *participate* in the idea of a period atmosphere. For instance, a martini bar would be a big hit at a 1950s style reception.

1910s

The sale of alcohol was still legal during the better half of this decade. Prohibition was instilled during the latter part of the decade which meant that people either stopped drinking altogether (which was hardly the case) or else hid the stuff they could get or make.

SINGAPORE SLING
One half-measure **gin**
One quarter **cherry brandy**
One quarter mixed **fruit juices** (orange, lime or lemon, pineapple)
A few drops of **cointreau** & **benedictine**
A dash of **angostura bitters**
Top with a **cherry** and a **slice of pineapple**.

FRENCH 75
2 oz. **sour mix** & **cognac**, chilled **champagne**
Stir **sour mix** & **cognac** in a collins glass with just a bit of ice, fill with **champagne**, garnish with a flag.
Substitute **gin** for the **cognac** & it becomes a champagne collins.

GIBSON
2 oz. **gin** or **vodka**, dash of **dry vermouth**
Stir with ice & strain into a chilled cocktail glass, garnish with skewered cocktail onions.

1920s/PROHIBITION

These cocktails either originated right before, during, or right after Prohibition. Pick a cocktail or a few of them to be served by the bartender along with any wine or champagne that might be on your list. Remember to give the bartender the recipes!

SIDECAR
2 ounces **brandy (cognac)**
1 ounce **cointreau**
½ ounce **lemon juice**
Shake with cracked ice.
Strain into frosted cocktail glass and serve.
Wet the rim of the glass with the **wedge of lemon**.
Coat the rim with **sugar**.
Garnish with a twist **lemon peel**.

STINGER
1 ounce **brandy**
¼ ounce **white crème de menthe**
Stir with cracked ice. Strain into chilled cocktail glass.
Garnish with **fresh mint sprigs**.
Serve with a glass of cold water.

OLD FASHIONED
2 oz. **whiskey** or **bourbon**, splash of **simple syrup**, **bitters** & **soda**
Fill rocks glass with ice, add **simple syrup**, **bitters**, **liquor** & **soda**. Garnish with **orange slice** and **cherry**.

MINT JULEP
2 oz. **bourbon**, dash of **simple syrup**, **mint**
Muddle **mint leaves** with **simple syrup**, add 1 oz. **bourbon**, fill with crushed ice, add rest of **bourbon**, garnish with a **sprig of fresh mint**.

1930s

THE CLASSIC MARTINI
1 1/2 ounces **gin**
1/2 ounce **dry vermouth**
Stir with cubed ice, strain into chilled cocktail glass.

JEAN HARLOW COCKTAIL
1/2 **bacardi rum**
1/2 **italian vermouth**
Peel or piece of lemon
Shake and strain into a cocktail glass.

PRESIDENT ROOSEVELT COCKTAIL
2 Dashes **grenadine**
1 Glass **bacardi rum**
Shake well and strain into a cocktail glass.

COSMOPOLITAN
1 1/2 oz. **vodka**, 1/2 oz. **cointreau** or **triple sec**, Splash of **lime juice** & **cranberry juice**
Shake with ice, serve in a chilled cocktail glass or on the rocks. Garnish with a **lime wedge**.

1940s & 1950s

MAI TAI
1 1/2 oz. **dark rum**, 1/2 oz. each: **orange curacao** & **creme de noyaux**, **lime juice**, **grenadine** (if desired)
Shake with ice and serve in hurricane glass.
Or add extra juice & blend with crushed ice for a frozen variation.
Garnish with an **orange slice** and a **cherry**.

BELLINI
1 ounce **white peach puree**
5 ounces chilled **champagne**
Pour **peach puree** into a champagne flute, then add **champagne**.

CHAMPAGNE COCKTAIL
Into each glass put a dash of **angostura bitters**, and a teaspoonful of **brandy**.
When ready, fill each glass with well-chilled **champagne cider**.
Serve right away.

VINTAGE MUSIC

Music is one of the most important elements that will help you create a period or vintage atmosphere. Music gets people up and dancing and involved in the entire event. The basic rule is to play period music during part of the reception with some variety of modern or Top 40 thrown in for guests that may not care for period music. Unless everyone at the reception likes period music, a variety of music ensures that some guests are not alienated.

You may also want to consider hiring a dance instructor to give a small dance lesson during the reception. A quick lesson in Charleston or swing will give your guests an excuse to get out of their seats and participate in the party. Make sure that the person you choose is qualified to teach and has a basic understanding of what types of dances were done during the decade you're wedding is based on.

Starting with 1920s music, you'll find that different version of the same songs remained popular for decades. It is important to make sure that who ever is providing the entertainment, is familiar with music from different decades. I've included a few artists with the songs to give you an idea of which version goes with each decade.

1910s SONG LIST

Ragtime was still popular and so were musicals. The songs of Irving Berlin, George Gershwin, and Al Jolson were also very popular. Below is a short list of some standard songs from the 1910s. Any good tango or waltz numbers also fit into the feel of a 1910s wedding reception.

When the Red, Red, Robin Comes Bop, Bop, Bopping Along

In the Good Old Summertime

Alexander's Ragtime Band

Danny Boy

You Made Me Love You

Ah! Sweet Mystery of Life

The Aba Daba Honeymoon

All I Do is Dream of You

1920s SONG LIST

Fascinatin' Rhythm - George and Ira Gershwin
The Man I Love - George and Ira Gershwin
Lady, Be Good - George and Ira Gershwin
It Had to Be You
Tea for Two
Sweet Georgia Brown
Always - Irving Berlin
Someone to Watch Over Me - George and Ira Gershwin
Blue Skies - Irving Berlin
My Blue Heaven - Gene Austin
The Varsity Drag
Me and My Shadow
Ain't She Sweet
Side by Side
'S Wonderful - George and Ira Gershwin
I Wanna Be Loved By You (Boop Boop-a-Doop)
I Can't Give You a Anything But Love
Let's Do It (Let's Fall in Love)
Makin' Whoopee
Frankie and Johnnie - Mae West
Star Dust - Hoagy Carmichael
Ain't Misbehavin'
Puttin' On the Ritz
What is this Thing Called Love?
Orange Blossom Time
Happy Days are Here Again
Nice Work If You Can Get It - George and Ira Gershwin

1930s SONG LIST

Body and Soul - Paul Whiteman
Bye Bye Blues - Bert Lown
Can This Be Love? - Arden-Ohman Orchestra
Happy Days Are Here Again - Benny Meroff
It Happened In Monterey - Paul Whiteman
My Baby Just Cares For Me - Ted Weems
On the Sunny Side Of the Street - Ted Lewis
Dream A Little Dream Of Me - Wayne King
Goodnight, Sweetheart - Guy Lombardo
Star Dust - Bing Crosby
All Of Me - Louis Armstrong
It's Only A Paper Moon - Paul Whiteman
Night and Day - Eddy Duchin
Sophisticated Lady - Duke Ellington
Stormy Weather - Duke Ellington
Try A Little Tenderness - Ted Lewis
Under A Blanket Of Blue - Don Bestor
Who's Afraid Of the Big Bad Wolf? - Ben Bernie
All I Do Is Dream Of You - Henry Busse
April In Paris - Freddy Martin
Continental - Jolly Coburn
Flying Down To Rio - Fred Astaire
Let's Fall In Love - Fred Rich
Moon Glow - Duke Ellington
Smoke Gets In Your Eyes - Emil Coleman
Stompin' At the Savoy - Chick Webb
Blue Moon - Benny Goodman
Broadway Rhythm - Guy Lombardo
Cheek To Cheek - The Boswell Sisters
I Won't Dance - Eddy Duchin
I'm In the Mood For Love - Louis Armstrong
Lovely To Look At - Eddy Duchin
Lullaby Of Broadway - Dorsey Brothers Orchestra
Lulu's Back In Town - Fats Waller
Solitude - Duke Ellington
Star Dust - Jimmie Lunceford
Top Hat, White Tie, and Tails - Fred Astaire

You Are My Lucky Star - Louis Armstrong
A Fine Romance - Billie Holiday
Goody Goody - Benny Goodman
I Can't Give You Anything But Love (Baby) -
Teddy Wilson featuring Billie Holiday
I'm Putting All My Eggs In One Basket - Fred Astaire
I've Got You Under My Skin - Hal Kemp
In the Chapel In the Moonlight - Shep Fields
Moon Glow - Benny Goodman
Organ Grinder's Swing - Benny Goodman
Pennies From Heaven - Bing Crosby
Star Dust - Tommy Dorsey
The Way You Look Tonight - Guy Lombardo
You Hit the Spot - Richard Himber
Gone With the Wind - Horace Heidt
Goodnight, My Love - Benny Goodman
The Love Bug Will Bite You - Jimmy Dorsey
Marie - Tommy Dorsey
Nice Work If You Can Get It - Shep Fields
Pennies From Heaven - Teddy Wilson with Billie Holiday
A Sailboat In the Moonlight - Billie Holiday
Stardust On the Moon - Tommy Dorsey
Stompin' At the Savoy - Benny Goodman
A-Tisket, A-Tasket - Ella Fitzgerald
Bei Mir Bist Du Schön - Benny Goodman
Flat Foot Floogey - Slim and Slam
I've Got A Date With A Dream - Benny Goodman
Lambeth Walk - Duke Ellington
Oh, Ma, Ma (The Butcher Boy) - Rudy Vallee
On the Sentimental Side - Bing Crosby
You Must Have Been A Beautiful Baby - Tommy Dorsey
Deep Purple - Guy Lombardo
Oh, Johnny, Oh Johnny, Oh - Orrin Tucker
Over the Rainbow - Judy Garland
You're A Sweet Little Headache - Benny Goodman

1940s SONG LIST

Apple Blossoms and Chapel Bells - Orrin Tucker
Blueberry Hill - Glenn Miller
Ferry Boat Serenade - Andrews Sisters
Frenesi - Artie Shaw
How High the Moon - Benny Goodman
Imagination - Glenn Miller
In the Mood - Glenn Miller
It's A Wonderful World - Charlie Barnet
Lover's Lullaby - Glen Gray
Our Love Affair - Tommy Dorsey
Pennsylvania 6-5000 - Glenn Miller
Pompton Turnpike - Charlie Barnet
There I Go - Vaughn Monroe
When You Wish Upon A Star - Guy Lombardo
Chattanooga Choo Choo - Glenn Miller
Intermezzo - Benny Goodman
Orange Blossom Lane - Glenn Miller
Perfidia (Tonight) - Xavier Cugat
Star Dust - Artie Shaw
For Me and My Gal - Judy Garland and Gene Kelly
Full Moon - Jimmy Dorsey
Jersey Bounce - Jimmy Dorsey
Sleepy Lagoon - Arty Shaw
The White Cliffs Of Dover - Glenn Miller
As Time Goes By - Rudy Vallee
Brazil - Xavier Cugat
Don't Get Around Much Anymore - Duke Ellington
Paper Doll - Mills Brothers
Praise the Lord and Pass the Ammunition - Kay Kyser
Taking A Chance On Love - Benny Goodman
Amor - Xavier Cugat
And Then You Kissed Me - Frank Sinatra

Bésame Mucho - Jimmy Dorsey
Do Nothin' Till You Hear From Me - Stan Kenton
G.I. Jive - Louis Jordan
Is You Is Or Is You Ain't (Ma Baby) ? - Louis Jordan
It Had To Be You - Artie Shaw
It's Love-Love-Love - Guy Lombardo
Shoo Shoo Baby - The Andrews Sisters
Swinging On A Star - Bing Crosby
Always - Guy Lombardo
Autumn Serenade - Harry James
I'm Beginning To See the Light - Ella Fitzgerald and
The Ink Spots
It's Only A Paper Moon - Benny Goodman
On the Atchison, Topeka, and Santa Fe - Tommy Dorsey
Sentimental Journey - Les Brown
Day By Day - Frank Sinatra
Hey Bop a Re Bop - Tex Beneke and the Glenn Miller
Orchestra
Linger In My Arms A Little Longer, Baby - Peggy Lee
Personality - Dinah Shore
Almost Like Being In Love - Frank Sinatra
An Apple Blossom Wedding - Eddy Howard
(I Love You) For Sentimental Reasons - Ella Fitzgerald
A Gal In Calico - Tex Beneke
Life Can Be Beautiful - Harry James
Zip-A-Dee-Doo-Dah - Johnny Mercer
It's Magic - Doris Day
Woody Woodpecker - Kay Kyser
Forever and Ever - Perry Como
Hop Scotch Polka - Guy Lombardo
The Hucklebuck - Tommy Dorsey
I've Got My Love To Keep Me Warm - Les Brown
Some Enchanted Evening - Frank Sinatra

1950s SONG LIST

Mr. Sandman - Chordettes
Sh-Boom - Crew Cuts
Shake Rattle and Roll - Big Joe Turner
Come On-a My House - Rosemary Clooney
Unforgettable - Nat King Cole
Rock Around The Clock - Bill Haley & the Comets
Earth Angel - The Penguins
Ain't That A Shame - Fats Domino
Only You - The Platters
Unchained Melody - Les Baxter
Cherry Pink and Apple Blossom White - Perez Prado
Love Me Tender - Elvis Presley
Great Pretender - The Platters
Blue Suede Shoes - Carl Perkins
Why Do Fools Fall In Love? - Frankie Lymon and
the Teenagers
Be-Bop-A-Lula - Gene Vincent
Tutti Frutti - Little Richard
Long Tall Sally - Little Richard
Don't Be Cruel - Elvis Presley
Hound Dog - Elvis Presley
See You Later Alligator - Bill Haley and the Comets
Whatever Will Be, Will Be (Que Sera, Sera) - Doris Day
I'm In Love Again/MyBlue Heaven - Fats Domino
Goodnight My Love - Jesse Belvins
Jailhouse Rock - Elvis Presley
Bye Bye Love - Everly Brothers
Peggy Sue - Buddy Holly
That'll Be The Day - Buddy Holly and The Crickets
Whole Lotta Shakin' Going On - Jerry Lee Lewis
You Send Me - Sam Cooke

Come Go With Me - The Del Vikings
All Shook Up - Elvis Presley
 (Let Me Be Your) Teddy Bear - Elvis Presley
Little Darlin' - The Diamonds
Keep Knockin' - Little Richard
Wake Up Little Susie - Everly Brothers
Day-O (The Banana Boat song) - Harry Belafonte
Rock and Roll Music - Chuck Berry
Be-Bop Baby/Have I Told You Lately That I Love You -
Ricky Nelson
Love is Strange - Mickey and Sylvia
At the Hop - Danny and the Juniors
Great Balls of Fire - Jerry Lee Lewis
Johnny B. Goode - Chuck Berry
Chantilly Lace - J.P. Richardson (The Big Bopper)
Tequila - The Champs
Splish Splash - Bobby Darin
Yakety Yak - The Coasters
Book of Love - The Monotones
Rebel Rouser - Duane Eddy
Tom Dooley - The Kingston Trio
To Know Him Is To Love Him - The Teddy Bears
Catch a Falling Star - Perry Como
Twilight Time - The Platters
Rockin Robin - Bobby Day
Who's Sorry Now? - Connie Francis
Tears on My Pillow - Little Anthony and The Imperials
Oh Boy - The Crickets
Purple People Eater - Sheb Wooley
Lollipop - The Chordettes
He's Got the Whole World in His Hands - Laurie London

CHAPTER 6
ODDS AND ENDS

WEDDING INVITATIONS

Period wedding invitations were quite plain and simple compared to what can be purchased today. They usually consisted of a nonfolding card invitation; reception invitation; and a reply card all embossed in black ink on ivory colored card stock. This look is classically simple and elegant. Be sure when choosing wedding invitations to choose a classic design and type face.

Mr. and Mrs. Grover Smith
announce the marriage of their daughter
Anna Smith
to
Mr. Andy Ray Griffith
on Saturday, the fifteenth of June
Nineteen hundred and forty
at four oclock in the afternoon
First Baptist Church
Flint, Michigan

Mr. and Mrs. Grover Smith
request the honor of
——————————— (NAME WRITTEN IN)
at the marriage of their daughter
Anna Smith
to
Mr. Andy Ray Griffith
on Saturday, the fifteenth of June
Nineteen hundred and forty
at four o'clock in the afternoon
First Baptist Church
Flint, Michigan

Mr. and Mrs. Grover Smith
request the honor of your presence
at the marriage of their daughter
Anna Smith
to
Mr. Andy Ray Griffith
on Saturday, the fifteenth of June
Nineteen hundred and forty
at four o'clock in the afternoon
First Baptist Church
Flint, Michigan

RECEPTION CARDS

Reception invitations should accompany the wedding invitation and should read as one of the following:

Mr. and Mrs. Grover Smith
request the pleasure of your company
immediately following the ceremony
780 Oak Street
Glendale, California
R.S.V.P

Reception
at four o'clock
Forty-six Lafayette Street

Mr. and Mrs. Grover Smith
request the pleasure of your company
Tuesday, the fifth of August
at five o'clock
780 Oak Street
Glendale, California
R.S.V.P

THANK YOU CARDS

Thank you cards are sent out to thank your guests for their wedding gift. These are sent out as soon as possible after you've received the gift. You may consider combining the "Thank you" card with the "at home" card on the next page.

Thank you
for your
Wedding Gift

Thank you
for your
Wedding Gift

Thank you
for your
Wedding Gift

Thank You

thank you

Thank You

THANK YOU

Thank You

"AT HOME" CARDS

The bride and groom generally did not live together before the marriage took place and only after the wedding and honeymoon were completed, would they move in together.

"At home" cards were to let friends and family know that the new bride was now ready to entertain visitors . These cards could be general invitations or have a specific time set aside for visitations. If you choose to send along an "at home" card, it should be included with the wedding invitation or with your thank you cards.

"At home" cards generally measure 3 ¼ inches wide by 2 ½ inches high. Fonts may be formal or more fun. If sending an "At home" card, choose one that best fits your life style so you do not encounter unexpected guests.

Please see examples below.

At Home
AFTER THE FIRST OF JANUARY
850 FIFTH AVENUE
MASON CITY, IOWA

Mrs. Dorothy Brand
will be at home
Tuesday, the eighth of December
from four until six o'clock
850 Fifth Avenue

Mrs. Dorothy Brand
at Home
Tuesday, the eighth of December
from four until six o'clock
850 Fifth Avenue

Mrs. Dorothy Brand

Tuesdays   15 West Terrace

Mr. and Mrs. John Cary
after the first of January
850 Fifth Avenue
Mason City, Iowa

Mr. and Mrs. John Cary

Tuesdays   15 West Terrace

BRIDAL CHECKLIST

❀ 1 YEAR IN ADVANCE

- Decide what type of wedding you would like.
- Decide on a budget.
- Pick a wedding date.
- Start thinking about your gown.

❀ 9-11 MONTHS IN ADVANCE

- Begin shopping for your gown.
- Visit potential wedding and/or reception sites.
- Finalize your wedding guest list.
- Choose attendants and groomsmen.
- Choose a color scheme.
- Decide on a caterer.
- Meet with the officiant.
- Book a band or DJ for the reception.

❀ 6-8 MONTHS IN ADVANCE

- Book ceremony musicians.
- Book a photographer and/or videographer.
- Book the baker that will be making your wedding cake.
- Decide on bridesmaids dresses and order them.

- Register for wedding gifts.
- Reserve hotel rooms for out of town guests.
- Order your wedding gown.
- Start planning the rehearsal dinner.
- Order wedding invitations and announcements.

❀ 4-5 MONTHS IN ADVANCE

- Groom decides what he and the groomsmen will be wearing.
- Start planning your honeymoon.
- Reserve tables, chairs, and any other rental equipment needed.
- Book rehearsal dinner site.
- Book hotel room for your wedding night.

❀ 2-3 MONTHS IN ADVANCE

- Decide on attendants' accessories (shoes, gloves, jewelry, etc.).
- Pick out or design a ketubah or other marriage contract required by your religion.
- Groom should supply groomsmen with all the information needed for them to reserve attire.

- Purchase wedding rings (if you have not already done so).
- Decide on specific ceremony items needed like a huppah, aisle runner, etc.
- Make sure that the attendants have purchased their dresses and accessories.
- Make or purchase favors to be given to guests at the reception.
- Purchase any special lingerie for the wedding gown before the first fitting.
- Groom and groomsmen should visit the formal wear shop to get fitted.
- Confirm delivery date of wedding gown and bridesmaids dresses.
- Get wedding rings engraved.
- Purchase veils and shoes before final dress fitting.
- Send out invitations.
- Arrange transportation for the wedding day.

6 WEEKS IN ADVANCE

- Arrange parking for reception if needed.
- Order alcohol if not included in catering cost.
- Confirm reservations for out of town guests.

- Write thank you notes for gifts received at bridal shower.
- Purchase guest book and nice pen.
- Groom has bachelor party.
- Bride has bachelorette party.
- Decide on a hairstylist.
- Bride should purchase gifts for attendants.
- Groom should purchase gifts for groomsmen.
- Final wedding gown fitting.
- Finalize vows.

3-4 WEEKS IN ADVANCE

- Design and print ceremony programs.
- Trial runs of makeup and hair.
- Send out invitations for rehearsal dinner.
- Discuss song preferences with ceremony musicians and reception entertainment.
- Pick up wedding rings and check the engravings.
- Purchase additional accessories like stockings, earrings, evening bag, etc.
- Final meeting with the officiant.
- Confirm honeymoon reservations.
- Get marriage license and blood test.
- Work out wedding-day time schedule.

- Purchase garter.
- Pick up the wedding gown.
- Plan a small party to thank your attendants for their help.
- Confirm delivery time and location with the cakemaker.
- Give final head count to caterer.

❀ 1-2 WEEKS IN ADVANCE

- Put together a seating chart and make place cards.
- Give a schedule to the officiant.
- Confirm delivery time and location with your florist.
- Groom should pick up his tux.
- Pack for honeymoon.
- Confirm final payment amounts with vendors.
- Confirm location, date, and time with photographer. Give them a "must take" photo list.
- Groom should get his final haircut.
- Put together an overnight bag.
- Designate someone to collect wedding gifts.
- Leave a copy of your honeymoon itinerary with someone in case of emergency.

- Put final payments and cash tips into marked enveloped and designate a person to distribute to vendors on wedding day.
- Confirm date, time, and location with wedding and reception musicians.
  Get a manicure and pedicure.

❀ DAY BEFORE

- Set your alarm and arrange for a backup call.
- Pull together wedding dress and all accessories.
- Have rehearsal dinner.
- Get sleep.
- Drop off guest book, pen, and favors at reception site if possible.

❀ DAY OF

- Tell your parents you love them.
- Get a massage.
- Exchange gifts and kisses with your fiancee.

❀ WHEN YOU GET BACK FROM THE HONEYMOON...

- Write thank you notes for gifts received.
- Freeze top layer of wedding cake.
- Get gown cleaned.
- Preserve your bridal bouquet.

VINTAGE WEDDING ANNIVERSARY GIFT LIST

FIRST: Cotton

SECOND: Paper

THIRD: Leather

FOURTH: Silk

FIFTH: Wood

SIXTH: Iron

SEVENTH: Wool

EIGHTH: Bronze

NINTH: Pottery

TENTH: Tin

TWELFTH: Silk and Linen

FIFTEENTH: Crystal

TWENTIETH: China

TWENTY-FIFTH: Silver

THIRTIETH: Pearl

THIRTY-FIFTH: Coral

FORTIETH: Ruby

FORTY-FIFTH: Sapphire

FIFTIETH: Gold

FIFTY-FIFTH: Emerald

SEVENTY-FIFTH: Diamond

HOW TO MAKE A NOSEGAY BOUQUET,
circa 1948

ABOVE. Inch-pleat twin ruffs of pink tarlatan four by eighteen inches long, wire ends like fan.

BELOW. Insert tip of five-inch length of florist's wire into calyx of rose to brace flower

3. LEFT. Cluster geranium leaves, spray of rose foliage around flower, secure with pipe cleaner.

4. RIGHT. Wire tarlatan ruff around nosegay, dot on household cement, sprinkle with glitter.

5. LEFT. Fragrant substitutes for flowers: sprigs of parsley, thyme, mint, verbena, rosemary.

Note: You can make mini-nosegays to be used as corsages.

APPENDICES

GLOSSARY

3/4 Length: A sleeve length that stops just below the elbow.

A

Accordion Pleats: Very close, small pleats.

Acetate: A fiber derived from cellulose. Dries more quickly than rayon.

A-Line Silhouette: Looks like a letter "A." Flatters most figure types.

Ankle Strap Shoes: A shoes that has a strap around the ankle.

Ascot: A scarf-like necktie with wide ends, worn around the neck, looped under the chin and held in place by a pin or tack.

B

Headpiece: A barrette, comb, flower(s), or bow that fasten to the head to which a veil is attached.

Ball Gown Silhouette: A fitted bodice with a bell shaped skirt.

Ballerina Length Skirt: A full skirt that reaches the lower calf.

Ballet or Waltz Veil: A veil length that falls between the knee and the ankle.

Ballet Slipper: A flat slipper usually made of satin.

Bandeau: A band worn across the forehead.

Basque Waistline: One of the most common bridal gown waistlines. Starts at the hips and comes down to a point in the center.

Bateau Neckline: A high, wide straight neckline that runs straight across the front and back, and meets at the shoulders.

Bertha Collar: A wide round collar covering the shoulders.

Blouson Bodice: Fullness of fabric from bodice to waist, very billowy, then cinched or gathered at or below the waist. Picture a peasant blouse. Popular with the dirndl skirt of the 1940s.

Blusher Veil: A short, single layer of veiling covering the face before the ceremony and lifted back over the head at some point during the ceremony. May be detachable.

Boater Hat: Circular straw hat with a flat top and straight brim. Commonly worn from late 19th century to the early 1940s. Picture a Barbershop quartet.

Boot: Men or women's footwear that covers the foot and part of the leg.

Bow Tie: A short necktie tied in a bowknot. May be worn with formal or semiformal wedding attire.

Box Pleat: A pleat with a squarish, flat front.

Brush or Sweep Train: This is the shortest of all trains and barely sweeps the floor while you walk.

Bustle: The draping of the train to keep it from dragging at the reception. Bustle may be an "over bustle" which is buttoned or hooked under the bow at the waist or a "French bustle" which is a combination of ribbon and loops tied together under the skirt.

Butterfly: A bow at the small of the back.

C

Cap Sleeve: A short sleeve that barely covers the shoulder

Capelet Sleeve: Flares several inches below the elbow.

Captoe: A men's dress shoe characterized by a toe that is capped in a different or same fabrication.

Cathedral Train: A train extending six to eight feet behind the gown. Used in very formal weddings. Also called a Monarch Train.

Cathedral Veil: The most formal veil style. Should be worn with a cathedral train in a very formal setting. Also called the Royal Veil.

Chapel Train: The most popular of all train lengths, it flows from three to four feet behind the gown.

Chapel Veil: A formal veil that extends to the floor. Should be worn with a formal gown that has a chapel or sweep train. May have multiple layers and/or a blusher veil.

Charmeuse: A satin fabric with a soft, lightweight and flexible finish.

Chemise Dress: A loose fitting, tube like dress.

Chiffon: A lustrous sheer fabric. Chiffon is lightweight and often layered.

Cloche: A close-fitting hat fashioned of straw, felt or cloth with or without a small brim that was popularized in the 1920s. Most appropriate for informal, garden or second weddings. Best worn with a suit or informal dress.

Clutch: A clutch purse is a handbag without straps. It has been popular throughout the Twentieth Century in various sizes and shapes, from the small beaded evening bag to the large envelope bag.

Comb Headpiece: A decorative piece that has combed teeth, to which a veil may be attached. Generally worn with an updo.

Coronet: A crown worn as a bridal headpiece,

Corselet: A wide, boned waistband used to cinch the waist.

Corset: A foundation garment. Usually a sleeveless form fitting boned bodice that either laces up or has snap closures.

Court or Square Neckline: A square neckline.

Court Train: Extends 1 yard from the waistline and is a little longer than the brush train.

Cowl: A piece of material attached at the neck, which may be draped loosely from shoulder to shoulder in the front or back. Think Grecian Goddess.

Crepe de Chine: Soft silk material.

Crossover Collar: A dress shirt collar with a lay down collar that crosses and fastens at center front. Commonly worn with a button cover.

Cuff Links: A decorative fastener that takes the place of a button at the wrist. Cuff links should be worn with the jewel face to the outside of the wrist. Cuff links are normally worn with French cuff shirt sleeves.

Cummerbund: A wide cloth band worn at the waist as a sash. Worn in place of a waistcoat for evening attire.

Cutaway Coat: A long jacket with skirts tapering from the front waistline to form tails at the back. Looks like a penguin shaped jacket. Also called a morning coat. Also called a morning coat.

D

Derby Hat: A hat with a high, round crown and an upturned brim. Most commonly a dress hat for men.

Dinner Jacket: A jacket appropriate for formal evening attire. Also called a tuxedo.

Double Breasted Coat: A coat having one half of the front lapped over the other having a double row of buttons and a single row of buttonholes.

Double Breasted Suit: A coat having one half of the front lapped over the other.

Double Tier Veil: A veil of two layers, usually of different lengths, one of which may be the blusher.

Drop Waistline: Falls 3-5 inches below the natural waistline.

E

Elbow Glove: Ends just above or below the elbow.

Elbow Length Veil: The elbow length veil should be used in an informal setting. May be up to 25 inches in length.

Empire Waistline: Falls right below the bust line and complements many figure types.

Evening Shoe: A slipper, sandal or pump that is fashioned in satin, shantung, brocade or patent leather. May be embellished with beading, stones or embroidery and is worn with evening wear or after-six apparel.

Extended or Royal Train: A train that is longer than four feet in length from the hemline.

F

Fedora: Soft felt hat with a tapered crown and a center crease.

Fingerless Glove: Fingers of the glove are absent.

Fingertip Veil: A veil that reaches the fingertips when arms are relaxed.

Fischu Collar: A woman's light triangular scarf that is draped over the shoulders and fastened in front.

Flannel: A classic suit material and one of the more comfortable to wear.

Flared Skirt: A skirt that is fitted at the waist and flares out in an A-line or tulip shape at the hem.

Flat Front Trousers: A trouser without pleats at the waist that lays flat over the abdomen.

Floor Length Gown: A gown lightly touching the floor on all sides.

Floppy Hat: A hat characterized by a wide brim that ruffles or flops down at the sides or front.

Flounce: A wide ruffle around the bottom of the skirt.

Flyaway Veil: A multi-layered veil that just brushes the shoulders This is less formal than other veil styles and may be worn with an ankle length gown.

Fountain Veil: A veil gathered at the crown of the head that cascades over the shoulders. Usually shoulder or elbow length.

Four-in-Hand Tie: A necktie tied in a slipknot with long ends overlapping vertically in front.

French Cuffs: Fancy shirt sleeves that require cuff links.

Frock Coat: A close fitting coat with a square bottom that reaches down to the knees. Very popular during 1910s.

G

Gabardine: A hard finished worsted twill fabric. It holds its shape and cleans well.

Girdle: A short corset reaching from the waist to the thighs.

H

Half Crown Headpiece: A half circle headpiece worn atop the head. Usually sits higher on the head than a tiara does.

Half Wreath Headpiece: A band of real flowers or foliage that is secured to the top of the head. Appropriate for less formal or garden weddings. May or may not be worn with a veil.

Halter Bodice: Collar or strap wrapped around the neck.

Head Band: A half circle band of uniform width that may be worn on top of the head.

Homburg: A felt hat with an indentation in the crown. Very similar to a Fedora.

I

Illusion Bodice: A gown with a yoke of sheer net fitting snugly around the neck for a choker effect. A satin band is sometimes used to accentuate the choker effect.

Intermission or Hi-Lo Skirt: The hem is shorter in the front and gets longer in the back. Popular in the late 1920s.

Inverted Basque Waistline: V-Shape is pointing up. Popular in the 1930s.

J

Jewel Neckline: A high, rounded neckline.

Juliet Cap: A small, round cap that fits snugly on top of the head.

K

Knee Length Gown: A skirt that ends at the knee.

L

Lace up Shoe: A dress or casual men's shoe that laces up.

Lay down Collar: Men's dress shirt with a turned down collar.

Long Sleeve: A sleeve that ends at the wrist.

Low Heel: Heel height between 1/2 and 1 inches.

M

Mantilla Veil: A circular piece of tulle or lace with lace edges draped over a comb. It is appropriate for both formal and semiformal weddings. May be any length in between elbow and ballet.

Medium Length Sleeve: A sleeve length that is just above or below the elbow.

Mermaid Silhouette: A slim, body-hugging dress with a skirt that flares out below the knee down to the floor. Very popular in the 1930s.

Mitts: Gloves starting a little below the middle of the forearm and coming to a point on the back of the hand. Popular in the early 1950s.

Morning Coat: *See Cutaway Coat*

N

Natural Waistline: Falls at the smallest part of the torso.

Nosegay: A round arrangement/bouquet of flowers. Generally small in size.

Notch Collar: A one or two-piece dress or coat collar.

Nylon: A fabric used in stockings, tulle, and menswear.

O

Off the Shoulder Neckline: May be short or long sleeved dropping 1 inch below the shoulders.

Open Toe Shoes: An opening at the toe of a sandal, pump or mule shoe.

Opera Glove: Extends to the upper part of the biceps and is appropriate for sleeveless or strapless dresses.

Organza: Fabric that is much like chiffon, but is heavier and stiffer.

P

Pannier Waistline: Draping of the skirt at the hips, similar to the classic peplum look. Creates an elegant, old-fashioned appearance.

Peak Collar: The peak is a two-piece lapel collar characterized by an upward peaked V-shaped lapel that attaches to the neckline collar.

Peplum: Short skirt sewn on to the bottom of a fitted bodice.

Peter Pan Collar: A high flat collar with rounded ends. Also called Buster Brown, Eton, or Dutch collar.

Picture Hat: A wide brimmed, round, shallow crowned hat that is embellished with tulle, netting, lace, flowers or beads. Popular in the 1910s.

Pique: A raised ribbed or honeycomb texture given to cotton fabric.

Pleated Trousers: A fold on either side of the fly front of the trouser waistline that adds fullness to the front of the trouser.

Pocket Squares: A pocket square is a square piece of silk, linen or synthetic fabric that is worn in the left hand breast pocket of a suit or tuxedo jacket. The pocket square is usually coordinated with the vest, cummerbund or tie.

Portrait Neckline: A shawl effect that wraps the shoulders.

Pouf Sleeve: May be short or long sleeve, gathered at the armhole and may end with a gathering into a cuff.

Pump: A closed toe, slip-on shoe that may be worn with suits, semiformal and formal attire. Characterized by a full enclosure of the foot and a medium to high heel.

Q

Queen Anne Neckline: High in back and sides, curving to a center point that resembles a heart-shape.

Queen Elizabeth Neckline: High collar that stands up in back and comes to a closed V in front.

R

Rayon: Originally called "artificial silk," this was the first man made fiber. It is made from cellulose.

Round Toe Shoe: A round shape on an enclosed toe shoe.

S

Sabrina Heel: A V-shaped heel that narrows at the bottom of the heel, inspired by the Audrey Hepburn film of the same name.

Sabrina Neckline: Straight neckline, slightly higher than bateau.

Sack Suit: A man's suit consisting of a jacket and trousers made of the same fabric. Appropriate for informal or daytime weddings. Popular in the 1910s and 1920s.

Sandal: An open-toed shoe characterized by straps across the toes.

Scoop Neckline: A low, rounded neckline.

Shawl Neckline: A one-piece collar that is turned down to form a continuous line from back to front.

Sheath Silhouette: A slim, body-hugging shape without a waistline. Popular in the 1920s.

Shirred Waist: Fabric is gathered to make a horizontal panel at waist.

Short Glove: Ends within two inches of the wrist line. Most appropriate for informal or semiformal events. Popular in the 1950s.

Short Sleeve: A sleeve length that comes to the middle of the upper arm.

Sleeveless: Exactly as you can imagine. Often seen with a bateau, boat, ballerina, or scoop neck.

Snood: Knitted net that is used to encase long hair at the back of the head.

Spaghetti Strap: A thin strap that attaches to the bodice.

Spats: Shoe coverings that reach up to the ankles, button or snap on the sides, and buckle underneath.

Stovepipe/Baggy Trousers: A pant leg that has added fullness.

Straight Skirt: Straight line skirt. Also called a pencil skirt

Strapless Neckline: Absence of sleeves and collar.

Street Length Skirt: A skirt hemmed to end just below the knee.

Studs: Decorative pins that fasten alongside buttons, replacing the standard button on men's shirts.

Suspenders: One of two supporting bands worn across the shoulders to support trousers.

Sweetheart Neckline: Heart shaped and may be strapless, bare or filled in with sheer netting. This is one of the most popular bridal gown necklines. Standard neckline for wedding dresses in the 1940s.

T

Taffeta: A stiff and heavy fabric often used in Bridal gowns and bridesmaid dresses.

Tailcoat: A man's full dress coat with two long tapering tails at the back. Appropriate for formal or very formal events.

Tapered Headband: A half circle band characterized by a wider middle and thinner or tapered ends, worn at the top of the head. Picture Cinderella.

Tea Length Skirt: A skirt that ends at the middle of the calf.

Tiara Headpiece: A jeweled or beaded semicircle worn on top of the head.

Tie Tack: A decorative pin that secures the holds an ascot or tie in place.

Tiered Skirt: A skirt comprised of layers of overlapping fabric.

Top Hat: A tall, high crowned hat usually of silk. Formal.

Triple Tiered Veil: A veil of three layers, usually of different lengths, one of which may be the blusher.

Trousseau: A collection of bridal belongings; wedding gown, lingerie, accessories, honeymoon wardrobe and even new household linens are considered to be part of a Bride's trousseau. Also called a hope chest.

Tulle: Fabric with a net-like appearance. Usually seen in veils and in the skirts of certain wedding gowns.

Tunic Overskirt: A blouse or bodice that is worn over another skirt. Popular during the 1920s.

Tuxedo: See Dinner Jacket.

Tuxedo Shoe: A dressy men's slip-on shoe usually fashioned in patent leather.

V

V-Neckline: Comes to a V in the front.

W

Waistcoat: A sleeveless, fitted garment that buttons at the center front with the hem normally hitting the waistline. Also called a vest.

Watteau Train: A train that attaches and falls from the shoulders. Also called a Capelet Train. Popular during the 1910s.

Wedding Band Neckline: A high collar that fits close to the neck for a very Victorian look. Popular during the 1910s.

Wing Collar: A starched, standing collar pointed turned back tabs. Also called dandy collar.

Wing Tip Shoe: Similar to a captoe shoes, a wing tip is a toe style characterized by an upward peak at the center point.

Wreath Headpiece: A circle of silk or real flowers that rests on the crown of the head. Appropriate for less formal or garden weddings. May or may not be worn with a veil.

Woolen: Fabrics that are softer and more loosely woven than worsteds. Includes tweeds, shetland, and flannel.

Worsted: Fabrics whose texture is smooth and clear. Includes serge, covert, or gabardine. Worsted fabrics drape and tailor well because of their smooth surface. They are resistant to dirt and wrinkle.

Y

Yoke: A yoke may either be the upper part of the bodice or a widened waistband to which the rest of the garment is attached.

NATIONAL GUIDE TO HISTORIC VENUES

Many of the hotels listed below are nationally renowned historic landmarks and are part of the National Register of historic places. Although this book is primarily concentrating on the 1910s-1950s, I've made a few exceptions by added some hotels that were so phenomenal that they deserved mention. Many of these hotels are perfect for weddings and receptions big or small, while others make for quaint and charming honeymoon getaways.

Alabama
RADISSON ADMIRAL SEMMES HOTEL – BUILT 1940
251 Government Street, Mobile
(334) 432-8000
Located in the heart of the historic district, this hotel contains an expansive marble floor in the lobby area with a curving staircase up to an oval balcony.

Arizona
ROYAL PALMS HOTEL AND CASITAS – BUILT 1929
5200 East Camelback Road, Pheonix
(602) 840-3610
This luxurious retreat was built by the nephew of J.P. Morgan as a summer house. Very Mediterranean in design, their expansive terracotta courtyards and gardens are great for a small outdoor wedding. This would also make an excellent honeymoon retreat.

California
ADAMSON HOUSE AND MALIBU LAGOON – Built 1929
23200 Pacific Coast Highway, Malibu
(310) 457-8185, Contact: Lynette Falk
The grounds are on the edge of the sandy beaches of Malibu. The area is available April to October, on Saturdays from 2 p.m. to 12 a.m., and on Sundays from 9 a.m. to 11 p.m. The maximum number of guests allowed is 200.

THE ALTA MIRA – BUILT 1920s
125 Bulkley, Sausalito 94966
(415) 332-1350
This is a 1920s hotel that had been fully restored. The facility has breathtaking views of San Francisco and the bay. Catering is provided.

ARCADIA HOUSE – Built 1930s
306 First Street, Arcadia 91006
(626) 447-0418, Contact: Scott Hart
This sixty-five year old Cape Cod style house has facilities for both indoor and outdoor functions.

AZTEC HOTEL – Built 1925
311 West Foothill Boulevard, Monrovia 91016
(626) 358-3231, Contact: Karen
When this Mayan Revival Hotel, it appeared in Ripley's "Believe it or Not." There is a lovely garden where wedding ceremonies are held. Adjoining it is a banquet room that has a beamed ceiling and French doors leading to a veranda.

BANNING HOUSE – Built 1910
P.O. Box 5044, Two Harbors, Santa Catalina Island 90704-5044
(310) 510-0303x228, Contact: Jacklyn Faris
The Banning House is situated on a hill overlooking Isthmus Cove and Catalina Harbor, and was used as a summer home. It is suggested that wedding parties reserve the entire lodge.

BEL-AIR HOTEL
701 Stone Canyon Road, Bel-Air 90077
(310) 472-1211, ext. 502 Contact: Deanna Maddalena or Rosemary Bamgemann
Beautiful outside gardens with trees, flowers, lake and swans are available for weddings and receptions. The gardens can accommodate a maximum of 160 people. Two rooms are suitable for weddings and receptions.

BRAZILIAN ROOM
Tilden Regional Park, Berkeley 94708
(510) 540-0220
This is a very popular wedding site and should be booked at least a year in advance.

BILTMORE HOTEL – Built 1923
506 South Grand Avenue, Los Angeles 90071-2607
(213) 624-1011, Contact: Steven Haller
The exterior is designed in the Italian Renaissance style. There are several elegant rooms available for parties: the Tiffany Room can accommodate 100; the Crystal Room 500-600 people; the Gold Room 250-300; and the Emerald Room can accommodate 250 people.

CALAMIGOS RANCH – Built late 1940s
327 South Latigo Canyon Road, Malibu, 90265
(818) 889-6280, Contact: Mon-Li or Pat
The 120-acre ranch was developed in the late 1940s by Grant and Helen Walter Gerson. The banquet rooms, featuring flagstone fireplaces and mountain views are attached to the patio area.

CALIFORNIA HERITAGE MUSEUM – Built 1894
2612 Main Street, Santa Monica 90405
(310) 392-8537, Contact: Tobi Smith
The entire museum and grounds are available from $1,000-$1,200. Up to 300+ guests can be accommodated on the outdoor grounds.

CASA ADOBE DE SAN RAFAEL – Built 1871
1330 Dorothy Drive, Glendale 91202
(818) 548-2147, Contact: Vicki or Jan
This home was built for Thomas Sanchez, the first sheriff of Los Angeles County. Weddings and receptions are held outside on the grounds.

CASTLE GREEN – Built 1897
www.castlegreen.com
99 South Raymond Avenue, Pasadena
(626) 793-0359, Contact: Stacy Ober,
The Castle is listed on the National Register of Historic Places and the National Archives of Significant Interiors.

CATALINA CASINO THEATER AND BALLROOM
Box 811, Avalon 90704
(310) 510-7400, Reservations: (310) 510-7404
A California landmark, this building combines historical glamour with Art Deco detail and architectural flair. It can accommodate groups of 200 to 1,800. The Descanso Beach Club is also available and can accommodating up to 2,000.

CHATEAU BRADBURY – Built 1912
Duarte 91010
(909) 595-8922, Contact: Andrea McCormick
This home was designed by the chief architect of the Pentagon in Washington D.C. It resembles a French Norman Chateau. You may use the ground floor of the mansion or the outdoor formal patio gardens.

CLARK ESTATE – Built 1919
10211 Pioneer Boulevard, Santa Fe Springs 90670,
(562) 868-3876 Contact: Tamara or Ophelia
Weddings and receptions are held on the spacious grounds, which has a courtyard with overlooking balconies at both ends, and a charming fountain front.

CRAVEN ESTATE – Built late 1920s
430 Madeline Drive, Pasadena 91105
(626) 799-0841 Contact: Diana Eyles; ext. 101
This is a French Chateau style home. An elegant entry hall, dining room, and living room are available for rental. French doors in the living room open onto a large patio and beautiful gardens.

DESCANSO GARDENS
1418 Descanso Drive, La Canada 91012
(818) 952-4400
These gardens are owned by the County of Los Angeles Department of Arboreta and Botanic Gardens. Receptions are held in the rose garden.

DEVONSHIRE HOUSE
18300 LeMarsh, Northridge 91325
(818) 349-7341, Contact: Adele
Clark Gable and Carol Lombard were the original owners of this house.

DUNSMUIR HOUSE AND GARDENS
2960 Peralta Oaks Court, Oakland 94605
(510) 562-0328
A breathtaking old house whose porch was made for wedding photographs.

THE DURFEE HOUSE – Built 1880
www.avictorianevent.com
1007 W. 24th Street, Los Angeles 90007
(213) 748-1996, Contact: Ann Dorr
The home features a beautiful garden setting and an elegant dining room, spacious living room and music room

EASTLAKE INN – Built 1887
1442 Kellam Avenue, Los Angeles 90026
(213) 482-5102, Contact: Murray Burns
There is an Greek revival temple outside the building which may be used for the wedding ceremony.

EDWARDS MANSION – BUILT 1890
2064 Orange Tree Lane, Redlands
(909) 793-2031
This is a beautifully restored Victorian mansion which includes a turn of the century wedding chapel, gazebo, tea garden, and water fall. They also offer a private Bridal suite with Jacuzzi. See photograph to right.

EL ENCANTO HOTEL AND GARDEN VILLAS – BUILT 1915
1900 Lasuen Road, Santa Barbara
(805) 687-5000
Known for their cottages and garden villas, this hotel has housed many Hollywood movie stars. Hedy Lamarr lived here for a short while. With serene garden settings and rooms with an ocean view, this makes a relaxing honeymoon spot.

FLEUR DE LIS CHAPEL – BUILT 1910
PO Box 1276
525 West 18th Street, Upland 91768
(909) 949-2227
If you want doves to be let go at your ceremony, use of this chapel includes them in the price. They also offer complete catering.

FOUNTAIN COURT RESTAURANT ASSISTANCE LEAGUE OF SOUTHERN CALIFORNIA
1370 North St. Andrews Place, Los Angeles 90028
(323) 856-0125, Contact: John or Gary
This building has a grand foyer with a curving staircase and a fountain-adorned patio. The Oval Dining Room can accommodate 220.

GARRATT MANSION
900 Union, Alameda 94501
(510) 521-4779
This is a very intimate setting for a wedding a reception. There is no ballroom, but makes up for it in charm.

GRAPEVINE ARBOR SAN GABRIEL CIVIC AUDITORIUM
320 South Mission Drive, San Gabriel 91776
(626) 308-2875 Contact: George Kotchnik
The famous Grapevine arbor which was planted in 1861, is housed at this location. Lawns and gardens provide the setting for weddings and receptions.

GREGG HOUSE – Built 1927
Altadena
(626) 398-8777, Contact: Greg Ross
This house is situated on an acre of gardens with rose bushes and arbors. Weddings and receptions take place outdoors.

GRIER-MUSSER MUSEUM – Built 1898
403 South Bonnie Brae, Los Angeles 90057
(213) 413-1814, Contact: Susan Tejada
The museum is suitable for small weddings (maximum 45 people). Weddings may take place in the front parlor with the rest of the ground floor available for a reception.

GRIFFITH PARK CLUB HOUSE – Built 1935
4730 Crystal Springs Drive, Los Angeles 90027
(323) 661-7212

HACIENDA HEIGHTS WOMEN'S CLUB – Built 1922
1917 South La Mecita Drive, P.O. Box 5565, Hacienda Heights 91745
(626) 968-4445
This is a beautiful building that can accommodate up to 150 guests. They also have a Fireplace Room, which can accommodate 25 people.

HAAS-LILIENTHAL HOUSE – BUILT 1886
2007 Franklin, San Francisco 94115
(415) 441-3011
This is a San Francisco landmark whose every room is an architectural treasure.

HOLLYWOOD ROOSEVELT HOTEL – Built 1927
7000 Hollywood Boulevard, Hollywood 90028
(323) 466-7000, Contact: Catering
This is a classic Spanish revival building that was designed by H.B. Travers. Their Blossom Room, which was the site of the first Academy Awards, is an elegant ballroom that seats up to 300 persons. They also have an Academy Room, which was the original home of the Academy of Motion Picture Arts and Sciences, and can accommodate up to 120.

HOTEL DEL CORONADO – BUILT 1888
1500 Orange Avenue, Coronado
(619) 435-6611
The Del has been filmed in many Hollywood Movies including *Some Like it Hot* with Marylin Monroe. The hotel is 15 minutes from San Diego and contains banquet rooms with an ocean view and outdoor setting for weddings.

HYATT SAINTE CLAIRE – BUILT 1926
302 South Market Street, San Jose
(408) 885-1234
This hotel has an outdoor patio with fountain which opens up into one of California's largest ballrooms.

INN ON MOUNT ADA – Built 1921
398 Wrigley Road, P.O. Box 2560, Avalon 90704
(310) 510-2030, Contact: Jan Donohoe
The inn has a large living room with antique furniture, baby grand piano, fireplace, and French doors which open to a terrace surrounding the front of the house. There is a breathtaking view of Avalon Bay and the mainland.

ITALIAN VILLA – Built 1925
336 Sturtevant Drive, Sierra Madre 91024
(213) 629-9222, Contact: Eva Malhotra
This home features stained glass windows, Gothic-arched hallways, Moroccan ceilings, Palladian windows, soaring ceilings, and magnificent views. The three-plus acres of grounds are covered with trees. Weddings and receptions can be held inside or out.

KOHL MANSION – Built 1914
2750 Adeline Drive, Burlinghame
(650) 992-4668
This rose brick, Tudor estate is situated on 40 oak filled acres and is surrounded by terraces, expansive lawns, and a historic rose garden. This is a beautiful wedding venue that is located just 12 miles south of San Francisco. You can fit more than one hundred guests in the Great Hall and the lawn south of the mansion is spectacular for afternoon receptions.

LA CASITA DEL ARROYO – Built 1933
177 South Arroyo Boulevard, Pasadena 91105-1075
(626) 794-0581, Contact: Mary Harley
The Casita consists of one large main room, kitchen, fireplace, tables, and chairs. Eighty is the maximum number of people allowed.

LA PLAYA HOTEL – Built 1904
Eighth at Camino Real, Carmel
(831) 624-6476
This Mansion was built as a wedding gift for a daughter of the Ghiradelli family. Situated on the coast in the cozy town of Carmel. The hotel includes formal garden, banquet rooms with views of the ocean, and a heated pool with gazebo.

LARK CREEK INN – Turn of the Century
234 Magnolia Avenue, Larkspur 94939
Touted as having the best food in Marin County. This is a great spot for an intimate indoor/outdoor wedding.

LA VALENCIA HOTEL – Built 1926
1132 Prospect Street, La Jolla
(858) 454-0771
This pink stucco, red tiled Mediterranean hotel overlooks La Jolla Cove and the Pacific Ocean.

LA VENTA INN – Built 1924
www.laventa.com
796 Via del Monte, Palos Verdes Estates 90274,
(310) 373-0123, Contact: Dante Angelos,
This is the Peninsula's oldest building. Wedding ceremonies are held on a terrace overlooking the ocean.

THE MAGIC CASTLE – Built 1908
7001 Franklin Avenue, Hollywood 90028
(323) 851-3442, Contact: Michael Fleming
This is a private club for magicians and is generally closed to the public, except for rental use.

THE MERMAID – Built 1930s
Topanga Canyon
(310) 455-1931, Contact: Bill Buerge
This home is situated in the Santa Monica Mountains and was originally built as a country club. The house was later used as gambling house for Mickey Cohen who stored slot machines in the basement.

MISSION INN – Built Between 1876 and 1931
3649 Mission Inn Avenue, Riverside
(909) 784-0300
This landmark takes up one entire city block. It contains a wedding chapel that has a 17th century gilded alter and an outdoor gazebo. Banquet facilities accommodate 10 to 200 guests.

NATIONAL MARITIME MUSEUM – Built late 1930s
Building 35, Fort Mason, San Francisco
(415) 561-6662
The building was constructed in the *art moderne* style to resemble an ocean liner. It is classic Art Deco style with terrazzo floors, murals, and chrome detailing. It has views of Hyde Pier, the Bay, and Alcatraz. Banquet facilities can accommodate up to 450 guests.

ORCUTT RANCH
23600 Roscoe Boulevard, West Hills 91304
(818) 346-7449, Contact: Cheryl Tabbi
This house is a California State Historic Monument. Weddings may take place in the courtyard area between the ranch house and rose garden. The ranch house can accommodate up to 100 guests.

OVIATT BUILDING – Built 1928
617 South Olive Street, Los Angeles
(213) 622-6096, Contact: Marina Bakits
This is beautiful Art Deco penthouse with a garden terrace. This is a very nice setting for an intimate wedding.

PASADENA MASONIC TEMPLE – Built 1926
200 South Euclid Avenue, Pasadena 91106
(626) 578-9776, Contact: Wallace Arntzen
This building has a beautiful marble foyer, large ballroom, dining room, and conference room. The ballroom holds 300 for dinner and dancing.

PETER STRAUSS RANCH
30000 Mulholland Highway, Agoura 91376
(818) 597-1036, ext. 223
This site has a large grassy area, small amphitheater, and an oak grove available for both weddings and receptions. The old ranch house on the property is off-limits.

QUEEN MARY HOTEL – Christened 1934
1126 Queens Highway, Long Beach 90802-6390
(562) 435-3511, Contact: Lovetta Kramer
The Queen Mary Royal Wedding Chapel is available for ceremonies. Up to 200 can be accommodated. Complete package plans and coordination is available.

SIERRA MADRE WOMENS CLUB (formerly Essick House) – Built 1911
550 West Sierra Madre Boulevard, Sierra Madre 91024
(626) 355-4379
This is a Craftsman Bungalow with a large living room, formal dining room, and garden pavilion. The site can accommodate up to 150 guests.

UNION STATION – Built 1939
800 North Alameda Street, Los Angeles 90012
(213) 625-5865, Contact: David Dickson @ Hollywood Locations (213) 742-0324
There are two indoor areas where weddings and receptions may take place.

VAN NUYS WOMAN'S CLUB – Built 1917
14836 Sylvan Street, Van Nuys 91411
(818) 997-9093
This is a Craftsman style clubhouse and can accommodate up to 200 guests.

WATTLES MANSION – Built 1907
1824 North Curson Avenue, Hollywood 90078
(213) 874-4005, Contact: Steve Sylvester
You may have your wedding or reception in the interior downstairs, on the front lawn, or on the terraced formal rear gardens. Valet parking is required, and all events must be over by 11 p.m.

WILLOW HEIGHTS MANSION
1978 Willow Springs Road, Morgan Hill 95037
(408) 778-1978
A beautiful old mansion located just south of San Jose.

WILSHIRE EBELL CLUB – Built 1927
743 South Lucerne Boulevard, Los Angeles 90005
(323) 937-6345
This is an elegant Italian Renaissance Club with a beautiful ballroom that is adjacent to a garden patio.

WOMEN'S TWENTIETH CENTURY CLUB – Built 1914
5105 Hermosa, Los Angeles 90004
(213) 256-9512, Contact: Ruth Genike
This is a historical landmark. It consists of a foyer, dining room, kitchen, and large room with a stage.

Colorado
THE BROWN PALACE HOTEL – Built 1892
321 Seventeenth Street, Denver
(303) 297-3111
This hotel features an eight-story stained glass atrium lobby and award winning cuisine.

THE OXFORD HOUSE – Built 1902
1600 Seventeenth Street, Denver
(303) 628-5400
This hotel was expanded in the 1930s and turned into an Art Deco showcase. The hotel has three ballrooms to choose from.

THE REDSTONE INN – Built 1902
82 Redstone Blvd., Redstone
(970) 963-2526
This hotel is a great example from the arts and crafts movement and is a one hour drive from Aspen.
The hotel has become a haven for many artists.

Connecticut
THE LIGHTHOUSE INN – Built 1902
6 Guthrie Place, New London
(860) 443-8411
A former Mediterranean mansion has had celebrities such as Bette Davis and Joan Crawford stay at the hotel. Includes a private beach and landscaped grounds.

Delaware
HOTEL DU PONT – Built 1913
11th and Market Streets, Wilmington
(302) 594-3100
Their marble and mosaic floors took over two years to complete and once finished, the hotel was proclaimed a rival to the finest hotels in Europe.

THE INN AT MONTCHANIN VILLAGE
Route 100 & Kirk Road, Montchanin
(302) 888-2133
Located halfway between New York and Washington D.C. in the heart of the Brandywine Valley, this little gem is great for a nearby honeymoon retreat.

Washington, DC
THE HAY-ADAMS HOTEL – Built 1927
16th & H Streets, NW
(202) 638-6600
The hotel is located across the street from the White House, and guests have included Amelia Earheart, Charles Lindberg, and Sinclair Lewis. The hotel has a seasonal rooftop terrace with views of the White House for private receptions.

THE JEFFERSON, A CAMBERLEY HOTEL – Built 1923
16th & M Streets, NW
(202) 347-2200
Originally an apartment building, then military housing during WWII, and finally a hotel.

RENAISSANCE MAYFLOWER HOTEL – Built 1925
1127 Connecticut Avenue, NW
(202) 347-3000
Includes a twenty-five foot skylight and murals. Banquet rooms can accommodate up to 1,000 guests.

Florida
THE BILTMORE HOTEL – Built 1926
1200 Anastasia Avenue, Coral Gables
(305) 445-1926
Contains three ballrooms, outdoor terraces, and expansive courtyards.

THE COLONY HOTEL AND CABANA CLUB – Built 1926
525 East Atlantic Avenue, Delray Beach
(561) 276-4123
Only open from November through April. Includes a private beach and one of the largest heated salt-water swimming pools in the area.

THE DON CESAR BEACH RESORT AND SPA – Built 1928
3400 Gulf Blvd., St. Pete Beach
(727) 360-1881
This is the historic "pink castle" that resides on Florida's west coast. Their ballroom has beach views and accommodates up to 420 guests.

RITZ PLAZA HOTEL – Built 1940s
1701 Collins Avenue, Miami Beach
(305) 534-3500
This is a first class, ocean front hotel located in the heart of the Art Deco district. Includes a grand ballroom with catering services.

Georgia
THE GEORGIAN TERRACE – Built 1911
659 Peachtree Lane, Atlanta
(404) 897-1991
Housed many celebrities and their grand ballroom hosted the *Gone With the Wind* world premiere party. The hotel also features a 19 story glass atrium. Facilities and meeting rooms can accomodate 40 to 500 guests.

GREYFIELD INN – Built 1900
Cumberland Island
(904) 261-6408
Only 30 people live on the island where this hotel is located. Furnished with antiques, this is the ultimate getaway – there are no phones, so forget about being disturbed.

JEKYLL ISLAND CLUB HOTEL – Built 1888
371 Riverview Drive, Jekyll Island
(912) 635-2600
The hotel is located on a barrier island off the coast of Georgia. This was a hunting retreat for America's richest families including the Rockefellers, Vanderbuilts, Astors, and the Morgans. The public areas are decorated in their original Victorian charm. The hotel has banquet accommodations for up to 400 guests.

Illinois
HOTEL BAKER – Built 1928
100 West Main Street, St. Charles
(630) 584-2100
This was known as the "Honeymoon Hotel" in the 30s and 40s. However, their river-front rose garden provides a perfect place for an outdoor wedding.

DEER PATH INN – Built 1929
255 East Illinois Road, Lake Forest
(847) 234-2280
An English Tudor style hotel that contains outdoor gardens available for weddings.

OMNI AMBASSADOR EAST – Built 1926
1301 North State Parkway, Chicago
(312) 787-7200
This hotel captures the opulence of the Gilded Age. Lavish reception facilities for up to 200 guests.

REGAL KNICKERBOCKER HOTEL – Built 1927
163 East Walton Place, Chicago
(312) 751-8100
The hotel's Crystal Ballroom has a 28 foot gilded gold ceiling and has the worlds largest lighted dance floor. Junior ballrooms are also available for smaller receptions.

Indiana

FRENCH LICK SPRINGS RESORT – Built 1902

8670 West State Road 56, French Lick

(812) 936-9300

Many celebrities have frequented this resort. Al Capone was a regular visitor and Franklin Roosevelt was locked in for the Democratic nomination in the Grand Colonnade Ballroom. Surrounding the hotel are lush gardens and verandas.

Iowa

HOTEL FORT DES MOINES – Built 1919

1000 Walnut Street, Des Moines

(515) 243-1161

Great staircase for photographs.

Kentucky

THE CAMBERLEY BROWN HOTEL – Built 1923

335 West Broadway, Louisville

(502) 583-1234

Opulent ballrooms accommodate up to 700 guests.

Louisiana

LE PAVILLON HOTEL – Built 1907

833 Poydras Street, New Orleans

(504) 581-3111

This place has a rooftop pool.

HOTEL MAISON DE VILLE AND THE AUDUBON COTTAGES – Built 1800

727 Rue Toulouse, New Orleans

(504) 561-5858

Located in the French Quarter, this hotel has private cottages and a beautiful courtyard. John James Audubon produced a portion of his *Birds of America* series while staying here. They also provide catering for up to 100 guests.

HOTEL MONTELEONE – Built 1886

214 Royal Street, New Orleans

(504) 523-3341

Filled with glittering chandeliers and polished marble floors.

RADISSON HOTEL BENTLEY – Built 1908

200 Desoto Street, Alexandria

(318) 448-9600

Was once called the "Biltmore of the Bayou." Interior marble, stained glass windows and domed ceilings make this a romantic wedding setting.

Maryland

KENT MANOR INN – Built 1820

500 Kent Manor Drive, Stevensville

(410) 643-5757

This hotel's 226 acre estate is situated on the waterfront of Chesapeake Bay. The hotel has a garden gazebo for outdoor weddings.

Massachusetts

BOSTON PARK PLAZA HOTEL – Built 1927

64 Arlington Street, Boston

(617) 426-2000

This hotel is adjacent to public gardens for outdoor weddings or an Imperial Ballroom

For indoor weddings and receptions.

CHATHAM BARS INN – Built 1914

297 Shore Road, Chatham, Cape Cod

(508) 945-0096

An elegant ocean front resort surrounded by gardens, water, and terraces. Past guests include Henry Ford and the Dutch royal family.

THE FAIRMONT COPLEY PLAZA – Built 1912

138 St. James Avenue, Boston

(617) 267-5300

The gilded ceilings are decorated with trompe l'oeil paintings of the sky and period antiques are common throughout the hotel.

HAWTHORNE HOTEL – Built 1920s

On the Common, Salem

(978) 744-4080

Their Hawthorne Ballroom is highlighted by 19 foot Palladian windows and can accommodate up to 350 guests.

Minnesota

THE SAINT PAUL HOTEL – Built 1910

350 Market Street, St. Paul

(651) 292-9292

This hotel is the epitome of turn of the century elegance. They have a complete in-house catering service.

Mississippi

RADISSON NATCHEZ EOLA – Built 1927

110 North Pearl Street, Natchez

(601) 445-6000

This hotel has a charming New Orleans-like courtyard and a ballroom that accommodates up to 400 guests.

Missouri
HYATT REGENCY ST. LOUIS AT UNION STATION
One Street Louis Union Station, St. Louis
(314) 231-1234
This historic train station has been turned into an elegant hotel. They have an 11 acre glass enclosed train shed complete with a 1½ acre lake.

THE POLLARD – Built 1893
2 North Broadway, Red Lodge
(406) 446-0001
The Sundance kid robbed the bank across the street from this hotel in 1987. The inn was also host to Buffalo Bill Cody and Calamity Jane. They have conference facilities for up to 65 guests.

New Hampshire
THE BALSAMS GRAND RESORT HOTEL – Built 1866
Lake Gloriette, Route 26, Dixville Notch
(603) 255-3400
This hotel is located high in the White Mountains just a few miles from Maine, Vermont, and Canada. Great for a winter or spring weddings.

New Jersey
SEAVIEW MARRIOT RESORT – Built 1912
401 South New York Road, Absecon
(609) 652-1800
Grace Kelly celebrated her 16th birthday at this resort. This resort is golfer's dream come true. Invite all your guests to stay for the weekend and play golf before having the wedding in the historic banquet space that accommodates up to 700 people.

New York
THE ALGONQUIN, A CAMBERLEY HOTEL – Built 1902
59 West 44th Street, New York
(212) 840-6800
This hotel was host to the legendary round table of the 1920s whose members included Dorothy Parker and Robert Benchley. They offer elegantly decorated rooms for weddings or private receptions.

LA BELLE EPOQUE BALLROOM – Built 1985
827 Broadway at East 12th Street
(212) 254-6436
The ballroom was built only 15 years ago but replicates turn of the century Paris. Original Art Nouveau fixtures, flooring, and an 1880 pewter top bar all add to the Parisian experience. They also carry a full array of vintage silver wear and linens to make your reception all the more authentic. *See sample menu to the right*

MOHONK MOUNTAIN HOUSE – Built 1869
Lake Mohonk, New Paltz
(914) 255-1000
Located at the top of a mountain and at the edge of a lake, this hotel spans late Victorian through the Arts and Crafts periods of architecture. The meeting areas are in Victorian décor.

THE PLAZA, NEW YORK – Built 1907
Fifth Avenue at Central Park South, New York
(212) 759-3000
This hotel is a charming 19 story Franch Renaissance "chateau." Their lovely Grand Ballroom accommodates up to 600 guests.

THE SAGAMORE – Built 1930
110 Sagamore Road, Bolton Landing
(518) 644-9400
This water front resort has a beautiful ballroom.

THE WALDORF ASTORIA – Built 1930s
301 Park Avenue, New York
(212) 355-3000
This hotel is an Art Deco masterpiece. Beautifully decorated, this hotel has many banquet options to choose from.

Ohio
OMNI NETHERLAND PLAZA – Built 1931
35 West Fifth Street, Cincinnati
(513) 421-9100
A beautiful Art Deco treasure decorated with Rookwood fountains and stylized murals. They contain elegant ballrooms for the most romantic wedding.

RENAISSANCE CLEVELAND HOTEL TOWER – Built 1918
24 Public Square, Cleveland
(216) 696-5600
This hotel has three ballrooms to choose from.

Oregon
THE GOVERNOR HOTEL – Built 1909
611 South West 10th Street, Portland
(503) 224-3400
Includes a high ceiling ballroom that can accommodate up to 650 guests.

Pennsylvania

THE HOTEL HERSHEY
Hotel Road, Hershey
(717) 533-2171
This is THE Hershey's chocolate hotel. Fountains, gardens, and banquet rooms allows any bride some flexibility.

PARK HYATT PHILADELPHIA AT THE BELLEVUE – Built 1902
Broad and Walnut, Philadelphia
(215) 893-1234
Their huge Grand Ballroom can accommodate up to 2,000 guests.

Rhode Island

THE INN AT NEWPORT BEACH – Built 1940
30 Wave Avenue, Middleton
(401) 846-0310
This hotel is on the waterfront. Their Atlantic Ballroom can accommodate up to 150 guests.

THE HOTEL VIKING – Built 1920s
One Bellevue Avenue, Newport
(401) 847-3300
This hotel is located at the top of "historic hill." They have two elegant ballrooms to choose from.

South Carolina

THE WESTIN FRANCIS MARION HOTEL – Built 1924
387 King Street, Charleston
(843) 722-0600
This hotel has two elegant historic ballrooms.

Tennessee

THE HERMITAGE HOTEL – Built 1910
231 Sixth Avenue, North, Nashville
(615) 244-3121
Famous visitors to this hotel include Gene Autry and Dinah Shore. The lobby has a three story arched ceiling with skylight. Their Grand Ballroom accommodates up to 300 guests.

Texas

THE DRISKILL – Built 1886
604 Brazos Street, Austin
(512) 474-5911
This hotel was built to be the frontier palace of the South. The hotel has floor to ceiling arched doorways and a magnificent Citadel Ballroom.

THE MENGER HOTEL – Built 1859
204 Alamo Plaza, San Antonio
(210) 223-4361
This hotel was built on the site of the first brewery in Texas and was the finest hotel west of the Mississippi River. It is located next to the Alamo and has a Ballroom that seats 750 and a tropical garden. People that have stayed here included Generals Lee and Grant and Presidents Taft and McKinley. Teddy Roosevelt was said to have recruited the Rough Riders in the Menger Bar.

STOCKYARDS HOTEL – Built 1906
109 E. Exchange Avenue, Ft. Worth
(817) 625-6427
This hotel is located in a historic district. They have an indoor/outdoor patio with bar for seating up to 60 people. Celebrities that have stayed at this hotel … Bonnie and Clyde, they even have a suite named after them.

THE STONELEIGH HOTEL – Built 1923
2927 Maple Avenue, Dallas
(214) 871-7111
This hotel has its own "celebrity" level decorated with 18th Century English mahogany furniture. With some sweet talk and honeymoon giggles, you might be able to get a room.

Utah

HISTORIC RADISSON SUITE HOTEL – Built 1927
2510 Washington Blvd., Ogden
(801) 627-1900
The Ballroom has features of a Florentine palace and can accommodate up to 400 guests.

Vermont

BASIN HARBOR CLUB – Built 1886
Basin Harbor Road, Vergennes
(802) 475-2311
Since opening, this hotel has been a summer getaway for people coming in from the city. The Club is made up of cottages right on the waterfront of Lake Champlain and has extensive gardens for strolling.

THE OLD TAVERN AT GRAFTON – Built 1788
Grafton
(802) 843-2231
This hotel was a regular stagecoach stop on the run from Boston to Montreal. Guests of the hotel include Ulysses S. Grant, Nathaniel Hawthorne, and Henry David Thoreau. The hotel has banquet accommodation for guests up to 125. They also have a natural pond for swimming and cross-country skiing during the snow season.

Virginia
THE JEFFERSON – Built 1895
Franklin and Adams Streets, Richmond
(804) 788-8000
The hotel opened on Halloween to host the wedding reception of Irene Langhorne Gibson…the Gibson Girl. The hotel has a 36 step grand staircase which some say inspired the staircase in *Gone With the Wind*. Banquet facilities can accommodate up to 400 guests.

WILLIAMSBURG INN – Built 1937
136 E. Francis Street, Williamsburg
(757) 229-1000
The hotel is located in the most extensively historically restored communities in the world. Although it is not the oldest community to be restored, it is one of the finest and most complete. The hotel contains a restored colonial home that is available for banquets.

Washington
MAYFLOWER PARK HOTEL – Built 1927
405 Olive Street, Seattle
(206) 623-8700
This is the oldest restored hotel in downtown Seattle.

PARADISE INN – Built 1917
Mt. Rainier National Park
(360) 569-2400
The inn is open form mid-May through early October. A historic honeymoon escape set in a secluded wilderness area.

ROSARIO RESORT – Built 1909
1400 Rosario Way, Eastsound
(360) 376-2222
The hotel was originally a mansion built as a family retreat. The estate is set on 30 acres that overlook Cascade Bay and can only be reached by ferry or seaplane. This is a beautiful and lush honeymoon retreat.

West Virginia
HISTORIC BLENNERHASSETT HOTEL – Built 1889
Fourth and Market Streets, Parkersburg
(304) 422-3131
Has the very popular Charleston Ballroom that can accommodate up to 300 guests.

THE GREENBRIER – 19th Century
White Sulphur Springs
(304) 536-1110
During the 19th Century this hotel was the summer vacation spot of choice and was used as an army hospital during WWII. A great resort with mineral baths, golfing, and a Land Rover Driving School.

Wisconsin
HOTEL METRO – Built 1936
411 East Mason Street, Milwaukee
(414) 272-1937
This is a very handsome Art Deco hotel. The hotel contains a ballroom that accommodates up to 120 guests.

THE PFISTER – Built 1893
424 East Wisconsin Avenue, Milwaukee
(414) 273-8222
When its doors opened it was touted as being the "Grand Hotel of the West." The hotel houses the world's largest collection of Victorian art. The hotel is also known for their luxurious Turkish baths.

RESOURCES

CORSETRY SHOPS

Le Corset
P.O. Box 42008
Los Angeles, CA 90042
323-254-5496
William Toro makes beautiful custom made
embroidered corsets. His specialty is bridal corsetry.

Dark Garden
www.darkgarden.net
321 Linden St.
San Francisco, CA. 94102
415 431-7684

B.R. Creations
Post Office Box 4201
Mountain View, California 94040
U.S.A.
Phone: (415)961-5354

Online Sources:
www.milkmade.com
www.vintage-elegance.com
www.deliciouscorsets.com

COSTUMERS
(professional Costume Designers and Pattern Makers)

Kathy Arellano – Sunland, CA
(818) 353-6253

Victoria Fisk Couture
626-282-0784
dovewings@earthlink.net
Victoria Fisk Couture specializes in period evening
and wedding gowns. Victoria's designs are absolutely
breathtaking and are reasonably priced. She is
wonderful to work with and can custom make or
adapt any design to suit your fancy. Definitely worth
looking into.

Jorge Avalos
2222 E. 4th Street
Long Beach, CA 90814
562-433-9112
Specializes in custom made men's suits based on
period patterns. Made the suits for Big Bad Voodoo
Daddy.

Revamp
782 Haight Street
San Francisco, CA
415-863-.8626.

Period Attire Dealers

Antique & Vintage Dress Gallery
www.antiquedress.com
PO Box 600353
Newtonville, MA 02460
781-891-9659
This is one of the largest vintage clothing sites on the web and they keep their stock constantly updated. They have a large supply of wedding attire for both men and women from Edwardian through 1950s. They also carry top hats, wax head pieces, tiaras, and a variety of lingerie items.

Cattle Kate
PO Box SP
Wilson, WY
307-733-7414
Cattle Kate offers turn of the century western wedding attire for men and women. Wedding dresses from the days when you could mail order the bride too. Send them $3.00 to get their full color catalogue.

The Cleveland Shop
11606 Detroit Ave.
Cleveland, OH 44102
216-228-9725
They carry vintage Bride and Grooms wear and vintage trousseau items.

Gulden & Brown Gowns
www.vintagegown.com or
www.gulden-brown.com
2201 Mohala Way
Honolulu, Hawaii 96822
808-737-4696
Gulden and Brown have some really amazing gowns and accessories from the twenties through the fifties. They carry some of the most beautiful 1930s dresses I've seen.

Jana Starr Antiques
www.janastarr.com
236 East 80th Street
New York, NY 10021
212-861-8256
Since its opening in 1976, this shop has remained an excellent source for antique wedding dresses, veils, headpieces, hankies and fans. They carry a variety of antique laces that can be purchased and used to restore your own dress. They also carry various trousseau items including hand embroidered lace tablecloths, napkins, hand towels, sheets, pillowcases, lace curtains, etc. see photo for example

Paris 1900
2703 Main Street
Santa Monica, CA 90405
310-396-0405
This shop has been around since 1976. Their stock consists of wedding gowns from Edwardian through 1930s, ladies garments, lace veils and headpieces, and various trousseau items.
They also have vintage flower girl dresses and accessories. In addition, they also carry vintage-style Jewelry, bags, ring bearer pillows, etc.

Online Sources:
www.vintagewedding.com
www.antiquedress.com
www.vintagebride.com
members.aol.com/gowns4you
bridesandjokers.com
www.neens.com
www.reminiscing.com
www.cameowedding.com

MILLINERY

Atelier Mela
P.O. Box 1057
Fullerton, CA 92835
714-255-1455
Mela makes gorgeous hats from nearly every period
imaginable. They are all hand made with exquisite
detail and care. Pricing is very reasonable.

Celeste
5971 3rd Street
Los Angeles, CA
323-938-0009
Specializes in custom design hats.

Davyne Dial Millinery
72 Montview Drive
Asheville, NC 28801
828-253-9115
Specializes in vintage wedding hat reproductions for
both Bride and Bridesmaids.

Ellen Christine Millinery
255 West 18th Street
New York, NY 10011
212-242-2457
Specializes in both vintage and custom made hats.
This is a quaint shop in New York city that you should
defiantly try and stop by to see.

Hatmonger
www.hatmonger.com
They produce romantic hats for women inspired by
vintage styles. Their hallmark is in the use of vintage
jewelry and fabrics. They can match colors and
customize sizing.

MISCELLANEOUS

Antique Treasures
1320 Weeks Road, NE
Cleveland, TN 37312
423-559-8436
Antique buttons, buckles, and jewelry.

Lagniappe Oaks Perfumery
www.laoaks.com
PO Box 5984
Thibodaux, LA 70302
504-447-oaks
Lagniappe Oaks Perfumery creates hand-blended
perfumes from turn of the century heirloom recipes.
Their fragrances are only carried in select boutiques
and smell of a femininity and softness that is not
found in modern perfumes. Use as a perfect floral
accent for any vintage wedding gown or as a
treasured bridesmaid's gift. Each perfume comes in a
drawstring clutch with its own historical gift card.
They also make fragrant soaps. Visit their website for
ordering information.

Remix
7605 ½ Beverly Blvd.
Los Angeles, CA 90036
323-936-6210
This is a wonderful store! They sell never worn shoes
from the 1920s on up. This is a great source for
authentic period men and women's shoes.

GET THE SCOOP!

Wanna find out about upcoming vintage living projects before anyone else?

Copy or tear off the bottom portion of this page and send it in to be included on our mailing list for FREE.

You'll get information and discounts on upcoming titles and don't worry ... we won't sell or give your info away.

YES, PLEASE PUT ME ON YOUR MAILING LIST!

NAME

_____

ADDRESS_____

EMAIL

_____

CUT OUT ALONG DOTTED LINE AND SEND TO:
STREAMLINE PRESS - RESEARCH DIVISION
2106 ALBURY AVENUE
LONG BEACH, CA 90815

☐ **ALL OF THE BELOW**

☐ **VICTORIAN BEAUTY AND HAIRSTYLES**
☐ **EDWARDIAN BEAUTY AND HAIRSTYLES**
☐ **1920S BEAUTY AND HAIRSTYLES**
☐ **1930S BEAUTY AND HAIRSTYLES**
☐ **1940S BEAUTY AND HAIRSTYLES**
☐ **1950S BEAUTY AND HAIRSTYLES**
☐ **OTHER ERAS BEAUTY AND**
  HAIRSTYLES PLEASE
  SPECIFY_____

☐ **VICTORIAN FASHION**
☐ **EDWARDIAN FASHION**
☐ **1920S FASHION**
☐ **1930S FASHION**
☐ **1940S FASHION**
☐ **1950S FASHION**
☐ **OTHER ERAS FASHION**
  PLEASE SPECIFY_____

☐ **OTHER NOT LISTED HERE. PLEASE SPECIFY:** _____

BOOK ID: VW200100001